Reading Concordances

CW00819242

Reading Concordances

An Introduction

John Sinclair

London • New York • Toronto • Sydney • Tokyo • Singapore
Hong Kong • Cape Town • Madrid • Paris • Amsterdam • Munich • Milan

PEARSON EDUCATION LIMITED

Head Office:
Edinburgh Gate
Harlow CM20 2JE
United Kingdom
Tel: +44 (0)1279 623623
Fax: +44 (0)1279 431059

London Office:
128 Long Acre
London WC2E 9AN
United Kingdom
Tel: +44 (0)20 7447 2000
Fax: +44 (0)20 7447 2170
Website: www.history-minds.com

First published in Great Britain in 2003

© Pearson Education Limited 2003

The right of John Sinclair to be identified as Author of this Work has been asserted by him in accordance with the Copyright, Designs and Patents Act 1988.

ISBN 0 582 29214 X

British Library Cataloguing in Publication Data
A CIP catalogue record for this book can be obtained from the British Library.

Library of Congress Cataloging in Publication Data
A CIP catalog record for this book can be obtained from the Library of Congress.

10 9 8 7 6 5 4 3 2 1

Typeset in 10/12pt Times by Graphicraft Limited, Hong Kong
Printed and bound in Malaysia

The Publishers' policy is to use paper manufactured from sustainable forests.

J. R. Firth

I would like this book to be read as a tribute to the memory of John Rupert Firth, 1890–1960, whose ideas made possible the study of lexis as part of the meaning-creating potential of language. He supervised my research in the session 1958–59 at the University of Edinburgh, and my first paper on lexis, "Beginning the study of lexis", was contributed to *In Memoriam J. R. Firth* (Bazell *et al.*, eds, Longman, 1966). I am proud to have spent much of my career working towards an ever greater understanding of Firth's concepts of language, using research techiques that were not available to him.

Contents

Preface

What this book tries to do

The main aim of this book is to introduce corpus work to students, researchers and workers in the language industries. If you work through it conscientiously, you should at the end be able:

(a) to interrogate a corpus in order to retrieve evidence that is relevant to a linguistic enquiry
(b) to manage and interpret the first results of your queries
(c) to refine your queries further until you have a neatly organised body of evidence to present as a report on your findings.

The emphasis is on the acquisition of practical skills rather than the exposition of theory. There are a large number of theoretical points made as we go along, mainly in the keys to the tasks, but they are not gathered and organised into a specific stance. At this point in the development of corpus study the priority is for people to get first-hand experience of working with corpora, to understand the enormous power of corpus evidence, and to learn how to interpret the evidence that comes from a corpus.

What's new in a corpus?

To many commentators, there is nothing much new in being able to access a corpus. It is, after all, just a large collection of texts. Texts – that is to say, samples of language in use – have not been very popular in the dominant linguistic fashions of the last half-century, but the older traditions of linguistics were based on the direct observation of speakers and writers in action. Today we have both returned to this tradition and moved on; we carefully study usage in a corpus, but instead of the field worker with notebook and mosquito net, there is now the office worker with corpus and technical support.

There are two main novelties in the modern way of studying language. One novelty is the amount of it that is available. Before the computer, linguists could only study small samples of language at a time because of the limitations of their powers of observation and their memories. Even scholars who relentlessly collected instances of usage all their lives only had a few examples of any particular pattern, and there was no way of telling what they had missed. The situation is almost the opposite with corpora, especially large corpora, where techniques have to be devised to control the often massive amount of evidence.

New skills, new thinking

Before large amounts of data were easily available, most of the generalisation had to be done by intuitive guesswork; pre-corpus linguists were not able to check their notions. The second novelty of the modern work with corpora is that the amount of variation in actual usage makes accurate generalisation rather difficult. The difference is often said to be between "top-down" and "bottom-up" approaches; starting from the "top" it is extremely difficult to arrive at a description that fits the facts of usage, while starting from the "bottom" it is not easy to formulate sufficiently general statements. However, the experience and intuition of the researcher are available in both approaches, and so the so-called "bottom-up" approach, properly conducted, is really a two-pronged attack on the data from the top and bottom simultaneously.

In this new way of studying language the researcher has to maintain control of a potentially large quantity of evidence while trying out generalisations, and this requires intellectual skills that have not traditionally been taught. Instead of just finding a well-known "rule" that is close to the patterns in the data, a corpus linguist has to look at the detailed, individual instances and has to be prepared to formulate a statement that may have a strong original element in it.

If you are going to use corpora thoroughly, you will have to be prepared to put aside some kinds of argument that you may well be taking for granted at present. For example, many linguists argue that if you find a single example that does not fit a generalisation you should discard the generalisation. This is just not valid in corpus work, because corpora record actual language in use, and so contain all sorts of variation and even error. Thousands of people over decades, all over the world, old and young, may contribute their language to a corpus, and it would be very strange if they all spoke exactly the same English.

So you have to hunt for general patterns among a mass of varying and sometimes even conflicting evidence, and put to one side any occasional lapses (but keep an eye on them in case they are the first signs of a new generalisation!).

The datafiles in this book are so small that the analysis often attempts to be comprehensive, and it will be clear in several of the tasks that a great amount of time and space is spent on tracking down one or two strange instances. In most research projects or applications these would probably just be ignored.

Other aims

The tasks that follow have been chosen from a large collection to show a broad range of language patterning, and so you can actually learn a lot about the lexical structure of English by going through them carefully. See the paragraph below about Structural Lexicology. At the end of the book is a glossary of all the terms that I use, with references to tasks that feature them; another route through the book would be via the glossary.

Background and design

This book has evolved over a decade, driven by its growing utility value. During this decade its subject matter, the study of language collected in a corpus, has moved from a position on the periphery of linguistic science to an area which has to be involved in any serious investigation of the nature and structure of language. Even if one's primary research interest is language in the mind, it is difficult nowadays to ignore the evidence that is increasingly available from corpora.

The origin of the book was a set of activities written for "distance" Masters students at the University of Birmingham. Whereas the full-time residential students at Birmingham were well provided for on the campus, with the growing collection known as The Bank of English, the modern-age students who worked in Seoul, Kyoto or the Malaysian jungle had no such resources and no teachers on hand for immediate consultation. I therefore devised a simple method of presentation which remains standard in most of the activities in this book.

Design features

Each section sets out a task that involves studying the way words pattern together in a corpus. Starting from the physical facts of letters, numbers and punctuation marks occurring in texts, each task gradually brings in the exercise of one's intuitions about the language and one's knowledge of it, leading to observations and insights that are simultaneously grounded in the evidence and are also important linguistic abstractions.

There are four components to each section:

1. A brief introduction.
2. A series of *questions* and *instructions* to retrieve linguistically relevant information from the data. Each numbered item is a *minitask*.
3. The *evidence*, in *datafiles*, which most often contain computer-generated CONCORDANCES but occasionally profiles of COLLOCATIONS. The collocational profiles are ordered according to the significance of the collocates as measured by their T-SCORE.
4. The *key*, which sets out my responses to the minitasks.

How to use this book

It is important to have the relevant datafile in front of you while working on a minitask, and this can become awkward because a book is necessarily divided into pages. One solution is to photocopy the datafiles, for which the publisher grants permission. The larger page size of the photocopy allows you to make notes as well. For those with easy access to the World Wide Web, I intend to replicate the datafiles on my website, and from time to time I hope to add simple data-handling tools, so that users will be able to avoid even the small amount of work there is in gathering the evidence from the instances provided.

The web address is that of The Tuscan Word Centre, http://www.twc.it From there a link will be provided to the location of the datafiles. If a login prompt is given, you should enter your email address as "user" and "concs02" as password. (Any correspondence about the website should be addressed to me – jms@twc.it – and not to the publisher.)

It is recommended that you work through the minitasks thoroughly and methodically, even if you appreciate early on the point that is being made. Take the minitasks one at a time, and prepare your response, then compare it with mine. If there is a substantial difference between the responses, search for a reason; perhaps we are using terminology differently, or perhaps our interpretation of some of the instances is different. Please do not assume that if your response is not the same as mine, you are wrong; during the long period of trialling that the book has gone through I have changed my position many times as a result of perceptions and arguments from other users. The keys are just the best responses that I can come up with at the time of writing.

Unfortunately I cannot anticipate the responses of readers, and I imagine that they will be many and varied. So where the next step depends on agreeing an analysis I have to ask you to accept mine in order to build on the early observations.

It is very easy to "cheat" and look at the key before you have tried the analysis yourself. I really think that this would be a waste of time, since the most valuable activity that the book stimulates is the reader's engagement with the data in tackling a theoretical or descriptive problem. I do not think there is any quicker way to understand how to read concordances.

Structural lexicology

Another approach to the material in the book is to use it as a course book for a course in structural lexicology. There is a great and growing interest in lexical structures nowadays, and the standard works on lexicology say very little about these crucially important patterns. This book should complement the familiar works on lexicology, which tend to concentrate on other areas of vocabulary study, such as morphology and the historical development of the vocabulary. This book has very little on patterns below the word, and only occasional glances at earlier stages of the language; on the other hand it deals with a large variety of meaningful patterns of word combination, which the traditional books keep away from.

Glossary

The starting point for such a course is the glossary at the end of the book, where I hope all the working terminology that you need for using the book is set out. It could also be used as the basis of a teaching unit; by ordering and clustering the main terms, a quick syllabus could be prepared, and it is a fairly easy matter to use the entries as exemplifications of the terms.

Task classification

The tasks are organised in two ways. They are divided into four groups according to the level of complexity of the task, and if you are new to corpus investigation it is a good idea to go through them in the order in which they appear. They are also classified roughly for theme, and so if you want to study all the tasks that feature the lexical item, you can retrieve them. All this information is given in the Contents.

Methodology

The tasks in this book are designed to share a common methodology, which is outlined here. In a book it is possible to show only the first few steps, but I hope that this is sufficient to motivate the reader to the pleasure of consulting a corpus at first hand, and so I have outlined the method below, in general terms. I recommend these procedures as a basic strategy for retrieving information from a corpus and evaluating it. They are the result of many years' experience of working with corpora and may seem deceptively simple, but they usually give good results.

The simplicity lies in the practical origins of the work, after years of trial and error. Corpora typically contain much more information than a human being can handle at any one time, and the investigator can easily get swamped in a large quantity of heterogeneous data. The technique, presented here, of taking successive small samples allows the investigator to keep control of the investigation, and to formulate explanations that are then cyclically tested and refined – or abandoned – as the evidence accumulates. The sequence of steps in the methodology does not vary much, although the content of the tasks in the book covers a wide range of topics in current lexicology. So the user becomes rapidly familiar with the procedures. This generates confidence in one's ability to handle a corpus, and transfers readily to "live" corpus investigations, where the methodology can be applied in a more flexible way. In several sections there is recourse to a second set of data to confirm or extend the results of examining the first set. This gives a little of the flavour of the real thing.

The normal starting point for a corpus investigation is the concordance, which from early days in computing has used the KWIC format, where instances of a chosen word or phrase (the NODE) are presented in a layout that aligns occurrences of the node vertically, but otherwise keeps them in the order in which they appear in the corpus. Only the first 25 or so usually appear in the window on the computer screen.

Small samples

For a quick overview of the patterning, it is usually advisable to call up an unbiased selection of lines from the whole concordance, and it is best to start with only a few (my normal practice is to start with just a screenful, unless I know in advance that I am likely to reject many of them, but even then I will choose a hundred at most). Then using whatever sorting facilities are available, the patterns can be brought out more clearly for inspection. At this point there are two alternatives available; one is to ask for another small selection, and the other is to refine the search on the basis of the evidence of the first sample.

The first alternative is better when you feel fairly sure that the small sample you have studied has instances of most of the main patterns that you are likely to find. Then what you need is to confirm this, get a clearer idea of the frequency of the various patterns and concentrate on the variation, seeking to classify it and circumscribe it. In such a case you should ask for a second sample from the same dataset as the first, and then another and then another, and so on until you are satisfied that most of the main patterns are evidenced in sufficient quantity. You may also find that the accumulation of evidence sheds light on some difficult areas. After several repetitions of this cycle you should find that each new sample adds nothing or very little to the accumulated description; by this time it is unlikely that you have missed anything of importance, and you can make summary statements about the way the meaning is constructed with reasonable confidence.

But sometimes even inspection of the very first selection leads to the need for some refinement of the data. Sometimes a query results in unexpected evidence, for example if a node word is also a common proper name, or it figures in a very frequent expression that you had not taken into account. It is usually possible to edit a concordance to remove unwanted material of this kind, but often this outcome shows patterns that lead immediately to the formulation of a refined query, and the procedure starts again.

Generalisation

In this book, the data is usually presented in the form of a single page of a concordance, sometimes in text order and sometimes sorted. This data is studied thoroughly on the assumption that it will probably show the main lines of the patterning of the node word or phrase. It is helpful to imagine that the data might be from a dead language, and that the small concordance is all the extant evidence of the use of a word or phrase. From this, the investigator must construct a description that is as predictive as possible, so that if another document turns up in the lost language, the description would have to be minimally amended.

To achieve a high predictability, some steps in abstraction and/or generalisation are required. It is well known in language text that sequences of words are rarely repeated exactly, but that there are often strong similarities among them that justify grouping them together, or strong differences that justify keeping them apart.

Obviously the investigator will use all the knowledge and intuition about the language that he or she has available, and will move from an examination of the physical evidence to some generalisations that group the data into sets which seem to show identical or sufficiently similar patterning in their environments.

Quite often the groupings will be reasonably familiar to anyone who knows the structure of English, and this is to be expected, since the normal statements about grammar and semantics will emerge and will be seen to be largely correct. Occasionally there will be a surprise.

"Degeneralisation"

However familiar the patterns of text may be, the investigator is encouraged to examine them closely, one by one. Sometimes the categories are much more restricted than a conventional description would provide, and sometimes they are considerably broader; also you may find words and phrases occurring together that are not normally associated structurally with each other.

Indeed, the investigator is encouraged to remain sceptical about "received" descriptions in general, and to pursue the patterns found in the data, because they may lead to more precise or alternative descriptions. Grammars and dictionaries are repositories of information that has been through an extended series of processes of selection and summarisation, during which a great deal of the evidence is lost, and the examination of corpus evidence may very well reveal information – important structural information – about the language which has never been written about in the literature.

Even today, very few published works have been able as yet to incorporate corpus evidence, and those that claim to have done so have often used corpora merely to support existing views about the language, and not used them critically. It is helpful to read carefully the statements in such publications about how corpus evidence is used.

So because of the powerful tradition of linguistic scholarship it is more than likely that anyone who has learned enough about language to be able to tackle a corpus has also absorbed a mass of theory, description and opinion about what to expect; language is exceptionally rich in patterning and if you are looking for something specific you will usually find it unless your reasoning and intuition have both deserted you. But in focusing on one pattern, you may fail to see another, much stronger and more important but not anticipated by previous authorities.

Hence the notion of *degeneralisation*. Your starting views on language are not merely those you have picked up in your education – everyone is competent in using at least one natural language and therefore has access to private language experience of great subtlety. People's views about language are often held most stubbornly, whether or not they are in accord with the facts that are available. For example, many people will swear that words which are different in spelling but identical in pronunciation (as far as can be observed with the most sensitive equipment) do sound different, or that the intonation pattern of an utterance goes up, when in fact it goes down. Problems of this kind can be tackled by breaking the link between the physical facts and the meaningful organisation of language, a kind of alienation technique.

So by composing early questions that are very earth-bound, like "which words are repeated immediately after an occurrence of X?", I help the user to decouple temporarily the powerful mechanism of generalisation and see a text as little more than marks on a page. Just to begin with, of course – the user will need a full complement of intuition and acquired knowledge to tackle later questions of classification and interpretation.

Procedural steps

I have had to think all the time of space and efficiency in preparing this book, but as you look through the sections you will be struck by the similarity of procedure. It is possible to outline a set of steps that should uncover the mysteries of most concordances, and I will try to do that here. In practice you should find that your intuition will guide you to shortcuts, but, looking ahead, it is clear that more and more of this methodical work will be done eventually by computer, and so there is need for a procedure which is reliable even if, to a human, needlessly laborious.

Step 1. *Initiate.* Look at the words that occur immediately to the right of the NODE. Note any that are repeated. Do the same with the words immediately to the left of the node. Decide on the "strongest" pattern and start there.

Deciding which is the strongest pattern depends on the circumstances, and with small numbers of instances is to some extent a matter of judgment. If one particular word form occurs in the same position in more than half the instances then it is pretty dominant, and is likely to be the best place to start; if there is no single word that stands out, but a grammatical word class is apparent in most of the lines, then start there. If there is nothing obvious at first sight, count which side has the largest number of repeated words; this is an indication of the coverage of repetitions, and a reliable place to start. Where you have strong patterns on both sides of the node it is safe to start on either side, since the retrieval of patterns is a cyclical procedure, and you will retrieve neglected patterns at Step 5.

Step 2. *Interpret.* Look at the repeated words, and try to form a hypothesis that may link them or most of them. For example, they may be from the same word class, or they may all have similar meanings.

Step 3. *Consolidate.* Assuming that Step 2 has been successful, now look for other evidence that can support the hypothesis – for example, single occurrences that come close to the criterion that you have set up, or structures that are different ways of expressing a similar meaning. Also you should look beyond the word position that you have started with, because there can be variations that separate elements of a pattern; look at the adjoining words and even some more distant ones, and in some cases also consider words on the other side of the node. Use always the criterion of how close they are to coming under the hypothesis that you have set up, and be prepared to revise and loosen up the hypothesis a little if by doing so you can include several more instances.

Examples of the sort of variants that occur are as follows. A pattern like "his N" can be stretched to include "Bill's N", or even "the N of the village". It can be developed into "his own N", pushing the two words apart, and even "his funny old N". The choice of active versus passive voice in grammar can alter the positions of words relative to each other, e.g. "they drove away in a bus" versus "the bus was driven away".

Step 4. *Report*. When you have exhausted the patterns you can observe, and have revised your hypothesis so that it is as flexible as it needs to be and as strong as it can be, write it out so that you have an explicit, testable version for the future. You will be surprised how often you may need to return to this and rephrase it without fundamentally altering the classification.

Step 5. *Recycle*. Now start with the next most important pattern in the vicinity of the node – probably on the other side from the first initiation. Go through the same steps as before, and after that look for the strongest pattern remaining on either side. Continue until you are not finding any repeated patterns, and then look at the remainder. If there are any instances that have not been cited as evidence for at least one hypothesis, examine them to see if they are unusual, or if there is something that this selection is not emphasising enough. If there are signs of an underlying pattern that has not been brought out by this selection, make a tentative note of it.

Step 6. *Result*. Make a final list of hypotheses and link them in a final report on the node that you started with.

Step 7. *Repeat*. Now gather a new selection from the corpus and start by applying your report to this new data. Go through the same steps, and confirm, extend or revise your hypotheses as you go along.

When to stop

After a few selections, depending on the complexity of the data, you will probably find that your hypotheses stand, and the only developments are additions to the lists of words and phrases that realise the categories. If your study is small-scale, this is a reasonable place to stop; if it is a more thorough study, then you can guess at some other words and phrases and look specifically for them. Grammars, thesauri and dictionaries can be useful here. If you get specific gaps, beware; there may be another factor operating that you had not noticed before. Check more closely.

It is unwise, though understandable, to try to examine each and every instance when the numbers are more than a hundred or two. Corpora – particularly large corpora – are designed for computers to do most of the routine work, and there is as yet no program that can take over your analysis at a certain point, check through all the rest of the evidence and complete an exhaustive description of your data.

Corpora and concordances

Unless stated otherwise, the concordance files in this book are selected from a corpus automatically. The number of instances in the corpus is divided by the number of instances required, and the result is used as the gap between selections; thus if there are 5000 instances of a word or phrase in the corpus, and 25 are required for the sample concordance, then the gap is $5000/25 = 200$. In text order, no. 1 is selected, then nos. 201, 401, 601, etc., until the 25th and last instance, no. 4801.

The concordance is silently tidied; duplicate examples, which occur quite naturally in collections of text, are omitted, obvious errors which do not affect the task are corrected, transcriptions of speech are regularised, and some signals which have been added by editors are taken out again. Any other changes or omissions are mentioned in the text.

The concordances used in the datafiles come mainly from the corpora at the University of Birmingham, from The Bank of English at various stage of its evolution.

Listings of collocates in this book (Sections 3, 12 and 18) are in order of significance, read vertically down the left-hand column, then down the second column, and so on.

References

Chomsky, N. (1957) *Syntactic Structures*. The Hague: Mouton.

Sinclair, J.M. *et al.* (1990) *Collins Cobuild English Grammar*. London: HarperCollins.

Sinclair, J.M. (1991) *Corpus, Concordance, Collocation*. Oxford: Oxford University Press.

Stubbs, M.W. (1995) "Collocations and semantic profiles", in *Functions of Language* 2.1.

Tognini Bonelli, E. (1992) " 'All I'm saying is' . . . The correlation of form and function in pseudo-cleft sentences", in *JLLC* 7.1.

Preface

Websites

Here are three useful "bookmark" websites for corpus linguistics; from these you should be able to find your way to the remarkable resources of the World Wide Web.

Michael Barlow: http://www.ruf.rice.edu/~barlow/corpus.html
Knut Hofland: http://www.hit.uib.no/icame.html
David Lee: http://www.devotedto.corpora

Page xix

Acknowledgements

It would be difficult to list all the people who have helped in the long period of preparation of this book, so I will group them together and highlight but a few. Well over two hundred students and participants in courses at The Tuscan Word Centre have worked through earlier versions of some of the tasks, and have reported on the clarity and utility of them; as a result all of the tasks have been revised many times over. Quite a few students have produced written critiques of tasks, which have helped immensely. For a time the University of Nottingham sent some of its master's students to TWC, and they wrote assignments arising from the tasks; I am grateful to Ron Carter for his support of this co-operation. Linda Pearce sent a detailed report on the very first set of tasks, and at a crucial stage of development, Anna Mauranen, now of Tampere University, came to Birmingham and worked through a first draft of about half of the tasks now gathered here.

The Bank of English is the corpus built and maintained jointly by the University of Birmingham and HarperCollins, publishers. I gratefully acknowledge their permission to make use of concordances and collocational profiles taken from that corpus.

I owe a particular debt of gratitude to my wife Elena Tognini Bonelli, many of whose ideas are inextricably tied in with my own in the book. Throughout the decade I have enjoyed her unlimited support and profited from her sharp-eyed criticism.

LEVEL 1

Task 1

How meanings are shown

A dictionary lists words and meanings, and you can see at a glance that most common words in the language have several meanings. It would be much easier to describe a language, and perhaps easier to learn and use it if each word always gave us the same meaning, but this is not the case. The very common verbs like "set", "run" and "take" have dozens of meanings – how does the user know which meaning is appropriate? Do we try all the meanings very quickly each time we hear or read the word and work out the most likely sense, or are there other clues?

If we study instances of usage, we find that the surrounding words and phrases help a lot in determining the meaning. Consider, for example, the concordance of the word <u>block</u> in the datafile **01_block.doc**.

1. Read each example in turn and work out its sense. Do not use a dictionary, but make notes on the meanings.

2. Group the meanings together wherever you can. If in doubt, put them together, so that you end up with a rather small number of senses.

3. Pick out the largest group. Compare your selection with the key.

4. What word classes are found in this group?

5. Do you recognise any phrases, phrasal verbs, idiomatic constructions or the like among the twelve?

6. A barrier can be a concrete physical object or a more abstract thing in politics or social life. Classify the "barrier" instances, taking care not to over-simplify; some instances may not be quite clear in the short context, and some may have a meaning that covers both the concrete and the abstract.

7. Pick out the instances with a physical meaning. Study the four or five words on either side of <u>block</u>, and make notes on any repeated patterns of grammar or vocabulary choice.

8. Try to fit the non-physical barriers into the same categories as are set up in answer to §7.

9. Select the next largest group of instances with the same sort of meaning. Check with the key, and then note any patterns in the surrounding words. Continue with the remaining meanings; do not be surprised if there is little regularity in the patterns when there are very few instances.

10. From the evidence of these examples, summarise the main meanings and uses of <u>block</u>.

Datafile 01_block.doc

1	on foot between the administration	block	and some cells can take up to 25
2	operations are moves designed to	block	enemy penetrations. The counter-
3	fee are variable. In 1985,	Block	filed 10 million tax returns,
4	the 16th Century, salt was used in	block	form and scraped off with a knife.
5	Zulu men for rural areas) and a road	block	had been set up by young men
6	Ltd. could also find itself on the	block	if Sir James Goldsmith succeeds in
7	the livery yard. Although the stable	block	is in darkness, she knows her own
8	cross as he led the crowd on a three-	block	march to police headquarters. He
9	deep pockets, and setting it upon a	block	of stone between himself and the
10	Next to the main assembly	block	of the shipyard in the Baltic port
11	you're a winner! Underneath each	block	of three numbers is a prize value.
12	The antagonists fasten onto and	block	off the receptors so that the
13	he would chase one leaf half a	block	or more with his blower, whereupon
14	a yodel, came echoing down from C-	block	's Two-tier. Bauman
15	his state partners would be able to	block	such a move. A Montedison spokesman
16	antagonists" he's developed which	block	the chemical signals small cell
17	or have clips or rings put on them to	block	them. Early techniques
18	blindfolded man cried out in the cell-	block	yard: about five guards surrounded
19	Minister, Nikolai Ryzhkov, was on the	block	yesterday, not that of Mr
20	effectively took itself off the	block	yesterday and announced a sweeping
21	appeared to be the main stumbling	block	. Yorkshire refused to comment on
22	off ALL THREE numbers in a single	block	you're a winner! Underneath
23	a landscape, the seascape doesn't	block	your sight; it extends beyond it.
24	a turning point in your life. Do not	block	your own good; ask for guidance.
25	Another is to go to extremes to	block	your neighbours out of your life,
26	and circumstances that appear to	block	your path. There is a certain
27	nationalists today said they will	block	Yugoslavia's border crossings with
28	see it by our eyes. Siegel: Down the	block	, Ziyad, who runs a souvenir shop

Task 1

Key

1 and 2. No key is provided. The meanings are discussed separately. Note, however, that if you have carried out these steps without serious problems, you have demonstrated that in a large number of instances only a few words on either side are enough guidance for you to pick out the relevant meaning.

3. In my analysis, there are twelve instances where block has to do with a barrier placed in the path of something. The twelve lines are nos. 2, 5, 12, 15, 16, 17, 21, 23, 24, 25, 26 and 27. Even if your view is different, please concentrate on these twelve for the purposes of demonstration.

4. Two; nos. 5 and 21 are nouns, the rest verbs.

5.

No.	Phrase	Comment
5	road block	common collocation – compound
12	block off	phrasal verb
21	stumbling block	idiomatic phrase
26	block your path	cliché

6.

No.	Meaning type	Comments
2	tactical	could also be interpreted as physical
5	physical	road block
12	physical	block off
15	tactical	could also be interpreted as physical, but unlikely
16	physical	chemical blocks are different from physical blocks, but are put together here
17	physical	clips or rings are physical restraints
21	figurative	familiar idiom, never used literally
23	physical	sight
24	figurative	mental blocks
25	figurative	mental blocks
26	figurative	could be physical, but normally refers to mental blocks
27	physical	border crossings

7.

No.	Part of speech	What is blocked – "route" or "travellers"	
5	noun	road	route
12	phrasal verb	receptors	travellers
16	verb in relative clause	chemical signals	travellers
17	infinitive	them	travellers
23	verb in negative phrase	sight	travellers
27	verb in modal phrase	border crossings	travellers

8.

No.	Part of speech	Route or travellers
2	infinitive	travellers
15	infinitive	travellers
21	noun	travellers
24	negative	travellers
25	infinitive	travellers
26	infinitive	route

9.

No.	Meaning	Comment
1	building	compound – administration block
3	proper name	
4	large lump	salt
6	execution	phrase – on the block
7	building	compound – stable block
8	town streets	measurement
9	large lump	stone
10	building	compound – assembly block
11	group of consecutive numbers	
13	town streets	measurement
14	building	compound – C-block
18	building	compound – cell-block
19	execution	phrase – on the block
20	avoiding execution	phrase – off the block
22	group of consecutive numbers	
28	town streets	location

Cases for comment

Numbers 1, 7, 10, 14 and 18 refer to buildings; in each case the noun is modified by another noun; two of these are hyphenated.

Numbers 8, 13 and 28 refer also to buildings, but to collections of buildings bounded by roads. Numbers 8 and 13 show this meaning in terms of measurement, and 28 uses <u>block</u> to mean the block where you live.

The phrase <u>on the block</u> occurs twice (nos. 6 and 19) with a meaning like "facing execution"; no. 20 may be similar, but is a little obscure.

The meaning of <u>block</u> as a large solid lump is found in nos. 4 and 9.

Numbers 11 and 22 mean a group of consecutive numbers.

One single meaning is no. 3: a proper name.

10. The word is principally used as a verb in the sense of placing an obstacle in the way of something. The object of the verb is usually whatever is being blocked, but it can also be the route. The verb has a wide range of objects, including people, vision, chemicals, and, in a more abstract sense, plans of action.

Noun uses of <u>block</u> carry several distinct meanings; while there is good evidence in the cotext to identify the most common one, there are too few instances of the others to be definite.

Task 2

Underlying regularity

Many uses of words in English are as parts of phrases. The meaning of the word is hardly separable from that of the phrase. As more and more evidence is gathered from corpora, this aspect of how words make meaning is growing in importance.

Phrases are the result of the co-ordinated selection of two or more words, and there is often a lot of variation in the way in the way a phrase can be made up. The actual words are not always fixed, and some do not always need to be present; the word order can also vary, and some words can vary in their inflections, while others appear only in one form in the phrase.

So on the surface of the language we tend to see a lot of variation; the regularities of phrases are often not obvious, because it is not often that exactly the same sequence of words recurs. We are aware of some repetition, but when we look carefully there always seems to be a lot of variation.

The computer allows us to gather together a lot of instances and makes them easy to compare, and see just what repetition and regularity there is.

There is a type of phrase which, although variable, includes a word that is confined to that phrase, and does not occur anywhere else in the language. A favourite example among linguists is the word *kith* in the phrase *kith and kin*. Whereas *kin* can be found in a number of different structures, and is a fairly free noun, *kith* only ever occurs in this phrase.

Another such word is *gamut*, and we will look at a sample of *gamut* in the datafile – see **02_gamut1.doc**. This is a rather uncommon word, with hardly any of its "own" meaning in current English. If you look up an old-fashioned dictionary, you may be told that *gamut* used to refer to a musical scale that had fourteen notes rather than the seven that is normal in the musical traditions of Europe – double the number in an octave. As you study the examples, consider if there is any of that meaning left in the phrase.

1. Make a list of the repeated words that occur immediately to the left of gamut. Sort them in frequency order. Then make a similar list of the words immediately to the right of gamut. Ignore single occurrences at present.

2. Look among the single occurrences to see if there are any which you think are small variations of one of the repeated words; provide a reason and revise the lists accordingly.

3. Now consider small variations of position. Look at the words at N–2, N+2, and make lists as in §1, then compare the lists with those you have made. Include single instances if they relate to the words that have already been repeated.

4. Review the variations so far. To the right of the node the patterns are remarkably fixed and we will return to them; to the left of the node there is some overlap between N–1 and N–2. Take each line in turn and see how they are distributed; in particular look for the combinations that occur, and attempt an explanation for them. Look beyond the second position where necessary.

5. Now look at the right-hand cotexts. Do you agree that they specify the area over which the phrase ranges? Do you notice anything about nos. 3–5, where from is the preposition?

6. Prepare a short account of the structure and meaning of the phrase around gamut.

7. If we choose the most likely word at each place in the phrase, what combination do we get? How many instances of this combination of choices are there in the concordance? Can you explain this finding?

8. Now turn to the second datafile, **02_gamut2.doc**. Repeat the analysis in §1–§6, noting any changes that you need to make with this new evidence.

9. This task has studied the nature of regularity and variation in phrases, and the way in which meaning is sometimes associated with a whole phrase rather than a single word. Summarise your findings.

Datafile 02_gamut1.doc

1	ng systems, the entire technological	gamut	, that we were at least their equal
2	up. We ran the usual conversational	gamut	, which centers around Old Stony's
3	sure. Well illustrated, it runs the	gamut	from gun making, gun fitting to gun
4	fore reaching conclusions. It runs a	gamut	from out-and-out materialism on one
5	powerful hands. Its snarls ran the	gamut	from pain to alarm, from alarm to o
6	uge curving mouth gave rise to a rich	gamut	of facial expressions which compleme
7	ing and beautiful things they run the	gamut	of texture from the sweet chestnut '
8	rt practices by re-examining the full	gamut	of expression which roots itself in
9	assed and re-passed through the whole	gamut	of American roadside restaurants, f
10	oke and iron and steel he had run the	gamut	of everything that could pierce and
11	Fathers can participate in the whole	gamut	of domestic work: shopping, food p
12	irshbaum stared at Gurewich. A whole	gamut	of feelings passed between them in t
13	ved difficult, she seemed to run the	gamut	of all the ills that babies can make
14	individuals who reflected the entire	gamut	of London politics from the Fabian s
15	they had run through practically the	gamut	of their vocabulary. Instead they p
16	be any common perspective amongst the	gamut	of structuralists from Lacan to Levi
17	has been squandered, and the whole	gamut	of opportunities that have been lost
18	ike mews of alarm. I heard the whole	gamut	on the mid-April day when, 35 feet

Datafile 02_gamut2.doc

1	habits of kids with cancer run the	gamut	from eating one banana a day and
2	patrons happy. Ginny soon runs the	gamut	from exhibitionism to self-
3	with the rest of the world run the	gamut	from outright condemnation to
4	indeed suspect. Its members run the	gamut	from reasonable-sounding chiefs to
5	make up the exhibition. They run the	gamut	from posters to holographs to
6	to use your gamut one? Well	gamut	occurs plenty in the
7	beyond this, however, and cover the	gamut	of physical and so-called mental
8	he went, and they ran the full	gamut	of his momentary preoccupations
9	and have usually been through a	gamut	of unsuccessful medical
10	explored her sexual appetites with a	gamut	of lovers – black, white, a
11	to exist in a co-operative, the whole	gamut	of training programmes had to be
12	shaped the ideas influencing a wide	gamut	of relations between the
13	viticulteur produces the full	gamut	of Alsace wines, including
14	and labour through the whole	gamut	of post-natal emotions
15	in Appendix 4). They run the whole	gamut	of investment choices, from very
16	corporatism and eventually the full	gamut	of Hitlerian ideas; and other
17	in "The Lake" she ran the	gamut	of emotions from A to B). Even so,
18	has made a major impact on the whole	gamut	of Network activities. While
19	days; and we get songs running the	gamut	of entertainment cliche. Consummate
20	Without this expert guidance, the	gamut	of amateur rug repairs often causes
21	chic, the season's variations run the	gamut	of styles and fabrics. At Dolce &
22	ago, Roselyn Turik has performed the	gamut	of keyboard works from baroque to
23	different locations and running the	gamut	of 20th century history form the
24	had a year ago. Yesterday, the whole	gamut	of the Russian press reflected
25	for ringing mystery prizes, the whole	gamut	. Then children's carousels, opening
26	but the profundity of feeling and the	gamut	. There's so much gaiety, there's
27	hour is usually enough for the whole	gamut	. This is Ireland after all, and the
28	programs, mind you, but the whole	gamut	. Unrepentant, he boldly asserted
29	but but they go they run the	gamut	you know. Mm. From you

Task 2

Key

1. We shall call <u>gamut</u> the NODE word, symbol N, and positions to the left of it N–1, N–2, etc. Positions to the right are N+1, N+2, etc. (see the glossary under SPAN for this notation).

Frequencies at N–1

the	7
whole	5

Frequencies at N+1

of	12
from	3

2. There is one instance of <u>a</u>, the indefinite article, which is an alternative choice to <u>the</u>. The words <u>entire</u> and <u>full</u> are very similar in meaning to <u>whole</u>, and <u>rich</u> shares some of the meaning that seems to be relevant in this phrasing. On the right-hand side there is no variation.

Revised frequencies at N–1

the/a	8
whole/entire/full/rich	8

3.

Frequencies at N–2

the/a	8
run/runs/ran	6
entire	
usual	

Frequencies at N+2

There are no repeated words in this position.

4. <u>Combinations</u>

All except the first two instances have <u>the</u> or <u>a</u> in one of these positions, and in those cases <u>the</u> is at N–3. Of the eight instances where <u>the</u> or <u>a</u> is at N–2, position N−1 has the word <u>whole</u> or similar. So there is a pattern to be seen, familiar in English grammar:

ARTICLE [ADJECTIVE] NOUN

Numbers 1 and 2 are a little more elaborate, having two adjectives; the first of these is of the <u>whole</u> set:

ARTICLE [ADJECTIVE − <u>whole</u>] [ADJECTIVE] NOUN

This formula summarises all the variation of the left side of the noun group, and all the occurrences at N−1. To continue the study of the noun group we turn to N+1 and observe that the first two instances are again different from the others, being followed in each case by a comma and a relative pronoun − the signs of the beginning of a non-defining relative clause and therefore the end of the noun group. We conclude provisionally that the second adjective in nos. 1 and 2 has a similar role to the prepositional phrases that follow the node in the other instances.

At N−2 there are six instances of a form of the verb "run", in each case followed by an article, and the pattern is found also at N−4 in no. 2. Similar verbs are found in no. 9 (<u>passed through</u>), no. 11 (<u>participate in</u>) and no. 15 (<u>run through</u>). The other verbs are <u>reflected</u>, <u>re-examining</u>, <u>gave rise to</u> and <u>heard</u>; these are more distant from the central meaning of the phrase. Three instances have no verb to the left, but no. 12 has the verb <u>passed</u> at N+3, which fits the general tendency.

An explanation of these patterns is that the phrase centring on <u>gamut</u> normally specifies an area over which it ranges; where this does not come after the noun it can be realised by an adjective of the "non-gradable" kind such as <u>technological</u> or <u>conversational</u>. Since the meaning includes a notion of a large range comprehensively covered, a modifier like <u>whole</u> reinforces that notion. The occurrence of the definite article before a noun followed by a prepositional phrase is normal; the preponderance of the verb <u>run</u> is idiomatic (here we may have a faint echo of the original meaning of <u>gamut</u>, since we often talk of "running" through musical exercises and pieces).

5. All but the last instance support this interpretation; in no. 18 the previous sentence is:

Listen, and you may hear a repertoire of calls that could make a mocking bird jealous, from hisses to hoots to catlike mews of alarm.

Clearly this is where the area is specified, and it is the <u>from</u> type.

Notice that <u>from</u> is followed by <u>to</u> shortly afterwards, specifying a range; this is also found in nos. 3 and 5, and if no. 4 is extended it is there too − but almost 50 words farther on!

6. The phrase typically consists of:

a verb – usually <u>run</u>, followed by
a noun group containing
    an article – usually <u>the</u>
    an adjective – usually <u>whole</u>
    the noun headword <u>gamut</u> and
    a prepositional phrase – usually <u>of</u> – which specifies the area over which the
    phrase ranges.

The adjective is optional. One variant is to omit the prepositional phrase and insert a second adjective specifying the range.

The function of the phrase is to specify some set of events, objects or tendencies, and to draw attention to the large size, fullness or complexity of the area concerned, the necessity for its contents to be enumerated one by one and the extensiveness of the coverage achieved.

7. The phrase made up word by word is:

run the whole gamut of . . .

There are no instances of just this phrase in the concordance. At this stage, with only 18 instances examined, the absence of this particular combination may be just a matter of chance; word by word it is the most likely one, and there are no obvious barriers to combination.

8. We repeat the procedures from §1–7.

Frequencies at N–1

the 14, a 2   total 16
whole 8, full 3, wide 1   total 12

Frequencies at N+1

of   18
from   5

Frequencies at N–2

the 11, a 1   total 12
run 6, running 2, runs 1, ran 1   total 10

Frequencies at N+2

There are no repeated words in this position.

Comment

The phrase pattern is confirmed, with even greater regularity. The set of adjectives led by whole is now:

whole, full, entire, wide, rich

Combinations

Of the five instances where the preposition is from, the following to is present. There is one instance (no. 15) of the phrase run the whole gamut of – so it is a possible combination, but a single instance is not good evidence of a settled pattern in the language.

Verbs other than "run" are cover, been through, and performed, which are similar to run, and influencing.

There are no instances of two adjectives between the article and the noun, but there are five instances – the last five – where gamut is not followed by an indicator of range. In nos. 25 and 28 the phrase refers back to a listing of range, and no. 27 is also anaphoric; but no. 26 is using gamut as an independent choice of noun, and 29 is a little obscure.

Number 6 shows gamut being cited as a word, dislocated from any cotext. This can happen to any word or phrase, and does not affect our analysis.

9. There is no more meaning in gamut than in ga, gam or gamu. Historically it once had a meaning, and some aspects of that meaning – e.g. the idea of a detailed enumeration of a long list – are still present. As always, there is a possible exception to this – in one instance (no. 26 of the second datafile) gamut refers to the compositions of Bach, and may be being used with some reference to its original sense.

Hardly any word except an article and gamut seems to be necessary, but the vast majority of the instances show the distinctive pattern that is set out in §6 above; the second datafile largely confirms the first one. The meaning of the phrase is also confirmed as it is set out in §6 above.

Task 3

Words as liabilities

A few years ago there was an interesting legal trial in south-east Asia, widely reported. A journalist writing about the politics of the region had used the word *regime* in reference to some of the governments of the region, without naming any. The government of the country where he lived felt that the use of this word about itself was insulting, and arrested the journalist and accused him of libel. The defence of the journalist was that he had not named his country of residence, and that the word *regime* was not so derogatory a reference as to justify a libel suit. Commentators (from a safe distance) recalled the English proverb "If the cap fits, wear it".

The government pursued its case and won a conviction. No-one asked a corpus linguist to give evidence of the word *regime*, and no-one came forward with text evidence of the way the word was used.

Imagine that you were on the jury for this case; on the assumption that the journalist had intended to imply that his government could reasonably be called a regime, make an assessment of the case against him.

1. Study the file **03_regime.doc**. Read each instance in turn, and select those where regime means government; note where it means something else. Look for words and phrases which could indicate a good or a bad SEMANTIC PROSODY, and put as many instances as possible in one category or the other, avoiding "neutral" whenever you can. Note what grammatical relationship each expression has with the node word regime.

2. Assess whether the good or the bad predominates; see how many of the others can be interpreted so as to join the main group. Make notes on doubtful decisions.

3. Now look at the file **03_regime_colls.doc**. There you will find the most significant collocates of regime, arranged by a measure known as T-SCORE. Put them into groups and summarise the kind of meaning that comes through.

4. Do you agree that if you call a government a regime you are likely to intend an insult to it?

Datafile 03_regime.doc

1	that Queensland has been seeking a	regime	which was not discriminatory and
2	the government as an apartheid	regime	. He maintained that with the steps
3	and leaving in place the appalling	regime	which these refugees from
4	the newest studio, a more benign	regime	prevailed, under the command of
5	at 40 as at 20, have an exercise	regime	to impress Jane Fonda, the perfect
6	the government probably prefer his	regime	to the theocracy favoured by a
7	Arab world, nobody could deny his	regime	's vigorous espousal of Arabism and
8	a godless and therefore illegitimate	regime	. Sociologists usually explain the
9	of a huge tariff. The new import	regime	has angered companies like Chiquita
10	now is whether and when the military	regime	will hand over power to a new
11	further discredited the military	regime	, which had shown by its
12	strong condemnation of the military	regime	. The Canadians are among those who
13	Dinitz, said he thought the new	regime	in Moscow would think carefully
14	Then London would deal with the new	regime	: until then it was bound to deal
15	to cross the threshold under the new	regime	." Geese nip out for love
16	changes if his twenty-year old	regime	is to survive. This month marks the
17	a "pseudo-state". 13 During the Old	Regime	, Spanish administration had a more
18	backs the boycott of the general's	regime	. According to Information, the
19	from both sides brought down the	regime	, and of course this was within the
20	counter-productive in terms of the	regime	's image abroad. Western men however
21	the Corriere has supported the	regime	with exemplary loyalty. '62 In the
22	groups in the provinces to staff the	regime	's political and ceremonial posts. 9
23	about the true nature of the	regime	. From that date, whatever illusions
24	of his bitter disillusion" with the	regime	only added to the sense of a
25	It exposes for what it is – the	regime	that we are dealing with, that we
26	at it, which is another side of the	regime	that everyone's known about, but no
27	the Bush administration to blast the	regime	publicly, in terms clear enough for
28	people in the country, because their	regime	killed hundreds of thousands of

Datafile 03_regime_colls.doc: the most frequent collocates of <u>regime</u>

communist	ancien	strict
new	Nazi	fascist
old	power	authoritarian
military	Baghdad	Mengistu
Iraqi	Soviet	collapse
Ceausescu	President	control
Saddam	Franco	Vichy
Hussein	dictated	repressive
Penh	overthrow	Kabul
Phnom	totalitarian	

Task 3

Key

1.

No.	Expression	Good/bad	Relationship
1	discriminatory	bad	complement
2	apartheid	bad	modifier
3	appalling	bad	modifier
4	benign	good	modifier (means management)
5			means "programme"
6	theocracy	bad	second object – regime is the first
7	vigorous espousal	good	regime's modifies
8	illegitimate	bad	modifier
9	angered	bad	verb with regime as subject
10	military	bad	modifier
11	discredited military	bad bad	verb with regime as object modifier
12	condemnation	bad	headword with regime in prep. phrase
	military	bad	modifier
13	new	neutral	modifier
14	new	neutral	modifier
15	new	neutral	modifier
16	changes	good	in main clause, regime in subordinate
17	pseudo-state	bad	previous sentence
18	boycott	bad	headword with regime in prep. phrase
19	brought down	bad	verb with regime as object
20	counter-productive	bad	headword with regime in prep. phrase
21	exemplary loyalty	good	in adverbial
22	ceremonial posts	neutral	regime's modifies
23	true nature	bad	headword with regime in prep. phrase
24	bitter disillusion	bad	in adverbial
25	exposes	bad	regime in apposition
26	known	neutral	in relative clause modifying regime
27	blast	bad	verb with regime as object
28	killed	bad	verb with regime as subject

2. In all but one instance, regime means government or some kind of managing authority. In 18 of these 27 instances the prosody is marked as "bad".

Instances marked "good"

- Number 4 has "a more benign regime prevailed", implying that the previous regime was malevolent.
- In no. 7, the attitude does seem to be good.
- In no. 16, changes have to be made, which implies that the regime is not good.
- Number 21 is probably ironical, since if regimes are on the whole bad, supporting them is also bad.

Doubtful decisions

- In no. 6, "theocracy" is not inherently bad, but a regime is preferred to it.
- Number 10 has <u>military</u> as a modifier; not all military regimes are bad, but since they are undemocratic many people would hold them to be bad in principle.
- In no. 17, the relation of <u>pseudo-state</u> to <u>regime</u> is not clear.
- In no. 23, there is also the word <u>illusions</u> to support the feeling that to reveal the <u>true nature</u> of something is to expose its bad side. I have been unable to find a single example of the collocation of <u>true nature</u> and <u>regime</u> that is even neutral, far less good in orientation.

Instances judged to be neutral

There are five of these. Three concern the word <u>new</u> as modifier, and it seems that this collocation counteracts the otherwise bad prosody of the word <u>regime</u>; also the regimes involved are often minor management roles, in sport for example, rather than governments. Number 22 concerns a dictatorship but presents it in a mild mode; the quoted line in no. 26 is just too short to show its menace – the text goes on to say that the regime is very dangerous.

To sum up this examination of the cotexts, we can say with confidence that almost all occurrences of <u>regime</u> bring out a bad prosody; the only systematic exceptions are those where <u>regime</u> is modified by <u>new</u>.

3. First there are some types of regime usually regarded as unpleasant among the sources of the corpus:

communist
Soviet
military
Nazi
fascist
totalitarian
authoritarian
strict
repressive

Then there is a "rogues' gallery" of dictators and their locations:

Ceausescu
Iraqi Saddam Hussein Baghdad
Franco
Mengistu
Vichy
Phnom Penh
Kabul

Next there are some words which offer further facets of meaning:

power
President
dictated
overthrow
collapse
control

Finally there are two familiar adjectives, and one fixed collocation, ancien regime – the only use of ancien in modern English. Regimes preceded by one of these three modifiers are unlikely to be nasty:

ancien
new
old

4. In summary, by far the greatest number of significant collocations of regime concern political systems and dictators with extremely unpopular reputations in the western world, or they concern the violent use of power.

Task 4

Literal and metaphorical

Some idiomatic phrases in English are recognisable because they contain a word which is not found anywhere else, like *at loggerheads*, *kith and kin* – see also Section 2, which deals with "gamut". Others are easily identified because their LITERAL meaning is absurd – see the introduction to Section 7 for some examples.

But many others have no such identification marks, and look and sound just like literal expressions – "He got cold feet", for example, seems quite a normal way of saying that his feet are cold. How then do we know when it means that he is cowardly?

This task studies a similar example, based around the collocation free hand. The datafile **04_freehand.doc** gives 30 instances, sorted alphabetically by the word immediately to the left of free.

1. Look at the words in this position (called N–1), and list them in order of frequency. Can you associate any of the SINGLETONS with any of those that recur?

2. Look again at the five lines where N–1 is an adverb of degree. What is the word at N–2? Then consider the two lines where N–1 is one. What is the word at N–2? Can you associate these seven lines with the two big groups of a and his . . . ? (See the Glossary under SPAN for an explanation of the position notation.)

3. We have now divided 28 of the 30 lines into two groups on the basis of the choice of DETERMINER in front of the noun hand. Grammars point out that there are two main types of determiner, one which tells us that the noun is identified, and the other which tells us the opposite. "The" is typical of the first type, and the possessive adjectives come in that group also; a/an is typical of the second type.

But here the difference is not just the type of determiner; consider the meaning of free hand in the two types of line and comment on the distinction in meaning.

4. What about the remaining two lines? This time start with their meaning – is it LITERAL or FIGURATIVE? Then see if there is any other evidence for fitting the lines into the groups.

5. Now we will look in more detail at the two groups of concordance lines, starting with those with a. Look at the word that comes before a. Again, list the words that occur in frequency order, and try to associate the singletons with the repeated words.

6. In the eight cases where the word in front of <u>a</u> is a noun or pronoun, look even further to the right, to the end of the noun group, and discover what the next word is. With this information, can you extend the description of the structures around <u>a free hand</u>?

7. Group the lines with <u>a free hand</u> according to the number of objects and whether the verb is active or passive. Does this explain why <u>given</u> occurs three times just in front of <u>a</u> but not at all otherwise?

8. From this information, put together a set of criteria in order to identify the figurative meaning of phrases that include <u>free hand</u>. Think of what a computer would have to look for.

9. We continue with this group of 19 lines, and see if there are any helpful regularities on the right-hand side. Start with the word at N+1, immediately after <u>hand</u>, and list the repeated words in frequency order.

10. In those cases where none of the repeated words occur at N+1, look further along the line to see if one eventually does; stop when you come to the end of a sentence or clause. Summarise the patterns to the right of the phrase.

11. Turn now to the other sense, and the other pattern, which we noted was marked by the occurrence of a possessive adjective at N−1. There are eight instances where this pattern occurs clearly: nos. 17–23 and 30. Look at N−2 or further to the left and note any repeated words or other patterns. Can no. 25 be added in easily here?

12. There are two lines left out of this analysis so far – nos. 11 and 28. Look at the cotext of each one, and consider its meaning; make a case separately for each line, as to whether it should be classified as one of the two meanings that we have identified so far, or whether it is different from both of them.

Datafile 04_freehand.doc

1	against allowing Western businesses a free hand to buy Russia's forests and
2	regional interests are: to have a free hand in Lebanon and to regain the
3	no doubt like to give the military a free hand but is wary of further
4	referred to as giving parents a free hand closing hospitals and
5	I says, "she thinks she's got a free hand . After all Claire
6	this instruction, he gave Stephanie a free hand in the decoration. Her main aim
7	and glows with pride in being given a free hand by the most influential
8	the army wants to be granted a free hand to crack down against the
9	gives President-elect Bill Clinton a free hand to shape the bank and thrift
10	is widely rumoured, have been given a free hand if they don't rock the boat on
11	boots. She brushed on makeup with a free hand cheeks like a clown, red mouth,
12	if financial deregulation gave them a free hand , bank managers would lend first
13	on the federal bench a judge has a free hand . A decade from now it may be
14	But Quayle denied Channel 9 had a free hand in nominating telecast
15	unlikely to give them a completely free hand in the matter. What Burma
16	er You've got a fairly free hand ? Yeah. Yeah.
17	was pointing down the road with her free hand . 'Look. The train's in. We'll
18	the rain had stopped. With his free hand he rolled down the window
19	resting on her shoulder. He moved his free hand around to the front of her
20	he yelled, but he grabbed her with his free hand , his fingers winding in her
21	the bottle against the palm of his free hand . He was a big man in his
22	at his chest with the thumb of his free hand . 'I don't care about you, I
23	health club, sir." He extended his free hand . 'A while ago. You'll maybe no"
24	wrist so tightly, she had only one free hand . Kelly pulled as hard as she
25	Nurse!" she shouted as with her one free hand she closed each window in turn,
26	allowing nature to have a relatively free hand . The spring garden, for
27	and he gives them a relatively free hand . They often abuse, they often
28	new broom will be brought in with the free hand to cut the dividend, clean out
29	setting. She was given a totally free hand by her clients to do exactly as
30	will only need the body brush so your free hand can be used to steady the horse'

Task 4

Key

1. a   14
   his   6
   relatively   2
   one   2
   Singletons:
   her, your – same word class as his
   completely, fairly, totally – same word class as relatively
   the

In half the instances the N–1 position is occupied by an article, almost always a; since the is the more frequent article generally, and occurs only once in this position, this pattern is a positive selection of the indefinite article, and a rejection of the definite article. In eight instances N–1 is a possessive adjective, mostly his; in five instances N–1 is an adverb of degree, twice relatively; in two instances N–1 is one.

2. Where N–1 is an adverb of degree, N–2 is a; so these five lines join the group of the indefinite article. Where N–1 is the word one, in no. 25 N–2 is her and so this line joins those with possessive adjectives.

The other one, no. 24, has only at N–2, which is unlike all the other lines in this sample, so we will fit it in later on.

3. Where the determiner of the noun group is a possessive adjective, the word free means "available", and the word hand means the part of the human body at the end of the arm. These are literal meanings. When the determiner is a, the phrase a free hand means "an unrestricted opportunity"; this is a figurative or idiomatic meaning.

4. Number 24 is clearly literal. In general with words like hand, denoting parts of the body that come in pairs (see eye in Section 18), reference specifically to just one of them is a literal reference.

Number 28 is a different matter, and as written it is very unusual. The clue is that it is the transcription of a spoken utterance. In fast speech the sound of "with the free hand" and "with a free hand" can be identical when the article is unstressed. When this phrase is transcribed, the transcriber has to make a choice of article, and this should be based on an examination of the COTEXT, using precisely the distinction in meaning that is given in §3. In my opinion the transcriber made the wrong guess in this instance.

5. The word in front of <u>a</u> is:

given	3
them	3
have	2
got	2

<u>Given</u> and <u>got</u> are verbs that have <u>a free hand</u> as object. This is also true of <u>granted</u> and <u>have</u>, <u>has</u> and <u>had</u>. That makes a total of ten of this type, out of nineteen, more than half. <u>Them</u> is a pronoun, and so takes the place of a noun group. Of the remaining words on our list, five – <u>businesses</u>, <u>military</u>, <u>parents</u>, <u>Stephanie</u> and <u>Clinton</u> – are nouns that either constitute the group by themselves (<u>parents</u>) or are heads of the group, e.g. <u>Western businesses</u>.

Only <u>with</u> in no. 11 is different, having a preposition in front of the phrase we are studying. We will return to this line later, but first read it carefully and judge whether it really is an example of the idiomatic meaning that goes with the selection of <u>a</u>.

6.	<u>give</u>	2
	<u>gave</u>	2
	<u>gives</u>	2
	<u>giving</u>	1
	<u>allowing</u>	1

These are all except one forms of the verb "give", which we have already seen is prominent in this lexical structure, and <u>allowing</u> is a form of a very similar verb to "give". So we see that there is a very particular choice of verb in this structure; of the nineteen examples, ten show "give" as the verb and two show verbs of similar meaning; six show <u>got</u> or a form of "have".

The verb "give", and others such as "grant" and "allow", can occur with both an indirect and a direct object; usually the first one is the indirect one, often a pronoun. Our phrase <u>a free hand</u> is the direct object. When the verb is passive, there is only a direct object – the pronoun or group that might have been the direct object is found as the subject.

7. Numbers 2, 5, 7, 8, 10, 13, 14, 16, 26 and 29 have only one object. Where the verb is "have" (nos. 2, 13, 14 and 26) only one object is possible and the passive is very rare; where the verb is <u>got</u> (nos. 5 and 16) an indirect object would be unusual and the passive would be ridiculous; in the other cases (nos. 7, 8, 10 and 29) the verb is "give" or "grant" and is passive.

Numbers 1, 3, 4, 6, 9, 12, 15 and 27 have two objects, and the verb is "give" apart from no. 1 where it is "allow".

8. (a) (i) Is there a form of the verb "give" to the left of the core phrase? or one from the same class and with a similar meaning?

(ii) If not, is there an occurrence of the verb "have" or "get", or one with a similar meaning and use?

(b) Does the indefinite article precede the core phrase, either directly or with only an adverb of degree in between?

If the answer is yes to both (a) and (b), the meaning is to be set a task without restrictions on resources or methods to accomplish it.

9. Repeated words at N+1:

in	4
to	3
by	2

10. In nos. 2 and 29 the infinitive marker to comes in later.

In summary, the patterns to the right are not very strong, but where the repeated words occur, in 11 – more than half – of the lines, they are confirming evidence of this meaning, because they are scarcely found in the other sense; no. 30 has an instance of the to-infinitive in the other sense, but that is all.

11. Repeated words at N–2:

with	3
of	2

In no. 22, with occurs at N–5 but is still part of the pattern.

Number 25 has with her one free hand, which is very close to the others and adds to the collocation of with. Numbers 19 and 23 have a verb of movement. None of these patterns occurred in our study of the figurative meaning, so this is useful, but not critical, evidence.

12. Number 11 seems at first sight to be a member of the figurative group because of the indefinite article; but the word at N–2 is with, which is strongly associated with the other meaning. So it is, in terms of cotext, balanced between the two. The meaning, also, has some association with each of the others. Hand comes close to referring to an actual physical object because the hands are used a lot in the application of make-up, and free is used more in its sense of "liberal" rather than as the opposite of "captive", though there is a bit of both present.

In fact the phrase with a free hand is a third phrase having free hand as it core; its combination of elements is different from either of the others although it uses the same words, and its meaning is distinct. The meaning is closer to the literal than our first sense, but is still figurative.

We come to this conclusion on the basis of only one concordance line, which means that it is almost entirely intuitive. It is predicting that there will be more instances of this kind, less frequent than the others but distinctive. The computer could be used to check this prediction.

Number 28 has already been noticed as unusual, because of its choice of the definite article (see §4). The meaning is certainly of the figurative type, but the structures do not fit the specifications that we have worked out. <u>Free hand</u> occurs after <u>with</u> in a prepositional phrase, which we associate with the literal meaning, and the verb is <u>brought in</u>, which we have not met before. This verb, however, is quite appropriate to the figurative meaning. We can also note that the right-hand side starts with <u>to</u> as an infinitive marker, which we have noted is characteristic of the figurative sense. So this instance shows that the cotext patterns are not "rules" which cannot be broken, but guides to normal phraseology.

Task 5

Meaning focus

Written language text takes the form of a string of words, with spaces in between. We tend to think that each word is independently chosen to deliver a meaning. For example, a noun like *houses* brings to mind the full range of someone's experience of houses; *stone houses* will now limit this concept to one particular variety of houses, those made of stone. The adjective *stone* is interpreted as selecting, from all the houses you can think of, houses that are made of stone.

In grammar this relationship is seen as the normal one between an adjective and a noun – the two words are separately chosen, and their combined meaning is the set of objects that share the two properties they express. In this task we shall examine whether such a relationship of meaning is the only one formed by combinations of adjective and noun, beginning with the adjective *physical*.

1. Look at the first datafile of *physical*, **05_physical1.doc**. This is a concordance that has been carefully selected to make a point, so please do not use it as a representative sample of the use of the word. Just consider what difference it makes in these instances to omit the word <u>physical</u>, and offer an explanation of your finding.

2. Now study the second datafile of *physical*, **05_physical2.doc**. First make a list of the nouns that immediately follow it. If the next word is not a noun, what is it, and can you find a suitable noun in the following few words?

3. In a few cases <u>physical</u> may have a scientific meaning, to do with the science of physics. Find these.

4. In the remaining items, first think of the meaning of the noun without looking at its cotext. Does it seem to you to have in itself the usual meaning of "physical"? If not, would you still normally expect that it will apply to physical events and things? Put the nouns into two groups according to your intuitions – aided by a dictionary if need be – and note any doubtful cases.

5. Now go through the concordance line by line, looking to see if the occurrence of <u>physical</u> narrows the referential range of the noun that follows, or draws attention to the essentially physical nature of the meaning of the noun in this cotext. In some instances there may not be enough cotext for you to be sure, and in such cases just guess. Make a note of discrepancies between your classification in §4 and the usage here.

6. Discuss the discrepancies noted in §4 and describe in summary the way the adjective <u>physical</u> is used in front of nouns.

7. The next step is to look at another adjective to see if it shows a similar pattern of meaning and use to *physical*. Study the datafile for *personal*, **05_personal.doc**. Pick out only those instances where there is a noun closely following, and then note any specialised uses, and how many there are. For the remainder decide in each instance whether it is focusing or selective. Point out any discrepancies with your intuitive idea of the meaning of the noun, and note any doubtful cases. Summarise the function of the adjective *personal*.

Datafile 05_physical1.doc

1 exercise and an increase in physical activity will protect bones, stimulate heart
2 the princess, who has been in frail physical health since suffering a mild stroke
3 There was no shortage of vigorous physical contact and skill. In recent weeks a
4 Gerald had been in peak physical condition. He was so fit and so healthy
5 whether your level of physical fitness is adequate for your present life-
6 These were rough, tough days where physical violence was not uncommon
7 right in believing that the physical presence of the United States troops in the
8 Give some thought to your physical appearance and the ways you might change it in
9 of the body. Descartes compared the physical body to a machine and suggested that
10 what they do reveal is that physical exercise can have a quite marked effect on
11 had also discovered his own physical strength and the damage he could cause with
12 that they were liable to cause physical damage to the vessel or its cargo

Datafile 05_physical2.doc

1	ers more than usually susceptible to	physical	injury is the fact that they never
2	They are visual warnings of possible	physical	attack by the person who is gestur
3	brain – stripped of its supporting	physical	structures – with the computer. I
4	tried to make up for their lack of	physical	stature by imposing themselves on
5	Detroit, also joined the team. The	physical	arrangement of the jail seemed to
6	signs are printed in skin colour or	physical	features. The colonial heritage,
7	them in terms of their spiritual and	physical	needs, then it becomes necessary
8	cle Sam might be suffering from some	physical	disease – he hinted at syphilis –
9	ue his way out of it. It was like a	physical	disease. He would tell himself,
10	ply. What he does is seek out those	physical	characteristics which make his sub
11	rld and about her position in it. A	physical	organism, of course, a distinct
12	urse war, with its accompaniment of	physical	destruction and social disturbance
13	a recurrent challenge – ineluctable	physical	and emotional demands – how it bro
14	concentration camp it resembles in	physical	outline, the people who live in i
15	ng that once upon a time there was a	physical	world devoid of life, this world
16	to quarrel about. The strained	physical	attitude to which she was clinging
17	boy babies more often get direct,	physical	expression of love and approval fr
18	heir home or lodgings address. 14 A	physical	recreation scheme, with a wide ve
19	east his book was written before his	physical	health deserted him, a book which
20	of passion, drama and intolerable	physical	loveliness that Ken Russell will s
21	personalities could also change the	physical	and chemical nature of our brains
22	omeone else at the wheel because her	physical	condition made it hard to drive.
23	ing and diarrhoea. As well as these	physical	problems, Lake, like hundreds of
24	ere people would be left at 'severe	physical	risk' would it be unreasonable to
25	eference to the likely inflicting of	physical	injury, and no mention is made of
26	the track. In her army mode as a	physical	-training instructor she would
27	is strict, with a lot of rigorous	physical	activity, the declared intention
28	over to children that exercise and	physical	activity can be enjoyable. They m
29	usually temporal, spatial and	physical	, but it goes beyond that. Some
30	ove legal tolerance for any level of	physical	punishment, in line with the UN C
31	formers who express complex ideas in	physical	language. It's tough but inspir
32	ds are circumvented by your superior	physical	prowess and overriding control. B
33	their periods, even if they have no	physical	problems themselves. So if these
34	there are vacancies for graduates in	physical	and computer sciences, engineerin

Datafile 05_personal.doc

1 | those of our guest writers are both | personal | and idiosyncratic. They're also
2 | a welcome stance on the need for | personal | and public morality. Now, John
3 | 03 July 1992 | PERSONAL | appearances are a lucrative source
4 | are finally aware that it is one's | personal | attributes and behaviour patterns
5 | running and on course to match her | personal | best, she would have just been
6 | we started to move towards using | personal | claim forms and now have the
7 | s death, and put notices in the | personal | columns of The Times
8 | Thomas A. Mays, 40, vice president, | personal | computer division, was named to
9 | letter was retrieved from Ayyad's | personal | computer by an electronics and
10 | only if you hold it in a tax-exempt | Personal | Equity Plan). Each carries, as a
11 | after last week's election, the | personal | fiefdom of its uncompromising
12 | trusts, taxes, and other aspects of | personal | finance. When a law firm, skilled
13 | private customers would use ' | personal | financial service centres' to deal
14 | Major General Bantu Holomisa, was a | personal | friend. But as the harmony in Dawn
15 | over misuse of public funds for | personal | gain. Mr Steinkuhler, who has
16 | in Bonn, albeit laced with | personal | grievances over their loss of
17 | to make love tonight. Express | personal | I think the meeting has opinion?
18 | at first. Mr Chissano resisted a | personal | meeting, fearing it would give the
19 | personal, part-political, but the | personal | ones were overriding. But
20 | Kenneth Kaunda has made known his | personal | opposition to the introduction of
21 | regaining office in November. The | personal | popularity of Jim Bolger has never
22 | power. I came to trust in my own | personal | power to do it. Now just about
23 | compare the features, taking your | personal | requirements into consideration,
24 | connection between women's fear of | personal | safety and gender roles (ibid., p.
25 | ideas as God, karma, revelation and | personal | salvation on the basis of personal
26 | that it is meaningful and more | personal | . So I think it – it will be a
27 | of teachers to the bishops as the | personal | successors of the apostles. This
28 | such clinics, clients can have | personal | supplies of the hormone shipped to
29 | of abortion and homosexuality are | personal | things and have no place in the
30 | if you've got a small amount for | personal | use you can actually laughing] get

Task 5

Key

1. The short answer is, nothing at all. Take no. 8 as a typical instance. All appearances are physical appearances, so whereas "stone houses" refers to a sub-class of houses <u>physical appearances</u> refers to the complete class of appearances. There are brick houses and wooden houses, but no "mental appearances".

So why is the word <u>physical</u> there at all? Its function is to focus attention on the physical meaning that is already in the noun; in the noun <u>appearances</u>, "physical" is one of many semantic features, not all of which are equally relevant to the particular instance. Many of the nouns in this concordance can be used in conjunction with an adjective like "mental" to give a non-physical meaning – even <u>body</u> can – and so the feature "physical" is suspended in such instances; by using the adjective apparently redundantly, as in this datafile, attention is drawn to that element of the meaning.

2. For the list of nouns immediately following <u>physical</u>, see §4.

Other structures

- Number 13 <u>and emotional demands</u>: two adjectives are linked together modifying <u>demands.</u>
- Number 21 <u>and chemical nature</u>: two adjectives are linked together modifying <u>nature.</u>
- Number 26 <u>-training instructor</u>: <u>physical</u> is part of a compound here, and this instance will be ignored from now on.
- Number 29 <u>, but</u>: <u>physical</u> does not immediately modify a noun in this instance.
- Number 34 <u>and computer sciences</u>: two adjectives are linked together modifying <u>sciences.</u>

Conclusion (ignoring no. 26)
In all instances except no. 29, there is a noun nearby which <u>physical</u> modifies.

3. In nos. 21 and 34 the word is linked by <u>and</u> to <u>chemical</u> and <u>computer</u> respectively, suggesting strongly that it is related to the science of physics.

4. Types of nouns.

(A) Nouns that contain the notion "physical":

destruction	disease	expression	health
injury	loveliness	organism	world

(B) Nouns that normally include the notion "physical":

activity   attack   condition
punishment   stature

(C) Nouns that can quite normally refer to non-physical things and events:

arrangement   attitude   characteristics   demands   features
language   outline   needs   problems   recreation
risk   structures

Notes

- It is possible to talk of "social disease", "mental injury", etc., but the point is that the adjective "social" or "mental" must be present to suspend the "physical" meaning. Another way of putting this is to say that these usages are metaphorical.
- The noun outline might be type B or even type A except in phrases like in outline, and its uses might refer to discourse and documents.

5. Where physical is selecting just part of the referential range of the noun, I will call it SELECTIVE (S). Where it is highlighting an aspect of the meaning of the noun, I will call it FOCUSING (F).

No.	Noun type (§4)	Function	Comments
1	A	F	
2	B	F	visual and gestur . . . support the physical interpretation
3	C	S	
4	B	F	most likely, though not certain
5	C	S	
6	C	F	printed and skin colour support the physical interpretation
7	C	S	antithesis with spiritual
8	A	F	S if the wider cotext mentions mental problems
9	A	S	it must be some non-physical disease
10	C	S	
11	A	F	not enough cotext to be sure
12	A	F	antithesis with social does not affect classification because each has its own noun
13	C	S	antithesis with emotional
14	C	S	
15	A	F	
16	C	S	
17	A	F	
18	C	S	
19	A	F	
20	A	F	a little doubtful without a wider cotext
22	B	F	this meaning of condition is perhaps A
23	C	S	likely contrast with other kinds of problems coming up
24	C	S	
25	A	F	

No.	Noun type (§4)	Function	Comments
27	B	F	not enough cotext to be sure, but strict and rigorous help
28	B	F	supported by exercise
30	B	S	other kinds of punishment are permitted
31	C	S	language perhaps should be type D – where the notion "physical" is in conflict with its normal semantic features
32	A	F	
33	C	S	

6. We would expect that physical with all type A nouns would be focusing, but one instance of disease is not, and the other is doubtful. The use of disease to refer to non-physical symptoms is still an unusual phrasing in English, and so the collocation physical disease is used for clarity in contrast with mental disturbances.

On the whole, physical with type B nouns should also be focusing, though more susceptible to selective interpretation. The only clear instance of select-ive meaning is no. 30, which appears to refer to legislation concerning the corporal punishment of children. Since other kinds of punishment are legitim-ate, physical is behaving in the same way as "stone" in "stone houses".

Physical modifying type C nouns can be expected to be selective, since there is no reason to expect the concrete notion "physical" to arise in the meaning of the noun. Number 6 presents an apparent counter-example, but perhaps the noun features has more than one meaning. Certainly the common meaning is extremely general and can apply to abstract ideas, but in the sense that goes with skin colour it refers to the shape etc. of parts of the human face, and thus perhaps should be reclassified as type A. See also condition in no. 22.

To summarise, the correspondence between types and usage is close, and the reasons for discrepancy are important.

(a) Collocation is a good guide to meaning, and when a noun is ambiguous in meaning (as many are) collocation can indicate which meaning is relevant. So nouns like features and condition have broad, general meanings of type C, but less common meanings of type A; when combined with physical the A meaning is the relevant one.

(b) Some stylistic structures create a contrast of meanings. One of them is the SIMILE, which says roughly "X is like Y". If X is like Y then X cannot actually be Y; and so when physical is placed as part of Y in a simile, as in no. 9, it must be selective even though the noun it modifies is type A. There are several reasons for creating such contrasts, and one is to project the meaning of a noun into an unusual combination, for example to sug-gest that a mental problem is as real and painful as an illness with physical symptoms.

7. There are three examples where there is no following noun; in nos. 1 and 26 the adjective is used PREDICATIVELY, and in no. 17 the passage is in note form.

Specialised uses

- Number 7. The Personal Column of *The Times* is a long-established section of that newspaper.
- Numbers 8 and 9. Personal computers or PCs are the familiar home and office machines.
- Number 10. A Personal Equity Plan is a kind of insurance policy.

No.	Function	Noun	Comments
2	S	morality	antithetical structure; noun is A-type
3	F	appearances	A-noun; all appearances are personal
4	F	attributes	A-noun
5	F	best	strong collocation, and best is not normally a noun
6	S	claim forms	contrast with some other kind of form
11	F	fiefdom	emphasises the power of the boss
12	S	finance	contrast with business financing
13	S	centres	same as 12
14	F	friend	A-noun stresses speaker's involvement
15	F	gain	see note below
16	F	grievances	not contrastive with other grievances
18	F	meeting	emphasises intimacy
19	S	ones	some "ones" are political
20	F	opposition	reinforces the personal element of his
21	F	popularity	A-noun
22	F	power	reinforces the personal element of my own
23	F	requirements	reinforces the personal element of your
24	F	safety	safety is person-oriented
25	F	salvation	salvation is person-oriented
27	F	successors	reference to the ceremony of consecration
28	F	supplies	draws attention to the privacy of the service
29	S	things	classifying
30	F	use	no contrast with non-personal use

Note on no. 15

Gain is an A-noun, so personal is clearly highlighting that aspect of its meaning. But it is also in an antithetical contrast with public. The fact that each adjective has its own noun allows the adjectives to contrast without forcing them to be selective. See no. 12 of 05_physical2.doc.

In several cases the adjective personal works with a possessive adjective that comes in front of it. The clearest cases are 20, 22 and 23, but there is some influence also in 4, 5 and 24.

Numbers

predicative	2 (nos. 1 and 26)
other non-attributive	1 (no. 17)
specialised	4 (nos. 7, 8, 9 and 10)
selective	6
focusing	<u>17</u>
	<u>30</u>

Conclusion

The adjective <u>personal</u> is used mainly in a focusing function.

LEVEL 2

Task 6

Specialised meaning

Most of the words in a language are uncommon; only a few hundred occur really often. Many of the uncommon words are restricted in meaning, and a large number are called "technical terms" because they are defined outside language texts, in a specialised discipline, and people who use them try to restrict their meanings to the definitions. Clearly, if a word keeps a pre-defined meaning it will behave independently of its context; the attempt is made to associate the word and meaning so closely that the meaning will not vary, regardless of the context of its use. This independence is possibly true of some very specialised terms, but it has not so far been proved, while it is known that language in use has an unpredictable effect on the words that are used.

This book takes its examples from general English, so there are only occasional references to technical terms. But there are still a lot of rare words – in fact one of the remarkable statistics of words in a corpus is that, no matter how large the corpora become, half of the word forms occur once only.

Some of these rare words name uncommon things in the world, and so they occur only on the rare occasions when these things are talked about. Others are restricted so much in their occurrence that they occur only in one or two idiomatic phrases – for an example in this book see the word "gamut" in Section 2.

But in this section we shall study another kind of uncommon word, one which has a clear cotextual pattern associated with it but is not thought of as part of an idiom. Why is it rare? Its meaning is clear, and indeed in all its occurrences it can be replaced by a more common word, and the same word in all cases. We might ask why it is in the language at all, if it is so unnecessary.

The likely answer, or part of it anyway, is that this word gives an extra flavour of meaning, more specific than a common word could be. It can be used precisely, and therefore economically. As will come clear, the special meaning is not easy to express in any other way.

The word chosen for this investigation is <u>brook</u>, used as a verb. To make a concordance of this usage it is necessary to separate the verbal uses of <u>brook</u> from the more common uses as a noun meaning a small stream. This is done by using a Word-class Tagger, but it has to be checked by hand afterwards. Since it is not a common word, we can study the complete concordance to <u>brook</u> in a fairly large corpus. This is printed in datafile **06_brook.doc**, with the words immediately after <u>brook</u> in alphabetical order.

1. List those words at N+1 (immediately to the right of <u>brook</u>) that are repeated. Is there any relation between them?

2. Check all the lines for evidence of negation. Look on both sides of <u>brook,</u> and note all the negative words. Can you formulate a simple general statement relating <u>brook</u> to the negative?

3. Now look at the word immediately to the left of <u>brook</u>, at position N−1, starting with nos. 11–36. Again, list the repeated words in frequency order. What is the predominant word-class? Can you fit any of the singletons into this word-class? (See the Glossary under SPAN for an explanation of the position notation.)

4. Expand your search to N−2, etc., and to the remaining lines (nos. 1–10 and 37–39). Can you find further instances of the predominant word-class? Can you see any words that have similar meanings to modals? What general conclusion can you come to about the relation of <u>brook</u> to modality?

5. Now we will look at what sorts of things people "will not brook" – that is, the objects of the verb. The easiest way to start is with the lines that have <u>any</u> or <u>no</u> at N−1 and to list the repeated words at N−2 in those lines. What kinds of words are they? Can any of the singletons can be associated with the repeated words?

6. Some of the instances have two nouns connected by <u>or</u>. Add in the other noun. Do they fit into the set we have built up from the N+1 words? At this stage bring in also the object nouns of the six lines we put on one side in §5 (nos. 7, 8, 9, 37, 38 and 39). Ask of all these words whether they are members of the set because of an inherent feature of their meaning or something caused by the local conditions.

7. We have studied the relation of <u>brook</u> as a verb with its objects; next we will have a look at the subjects. Who or what will not brook such things as interference? There are unlikely to be many repeated words here, because it is a fairly open choice, but try to group the subject nouns (the headwords of the subject noun groups) according to any shared features that you detect. Where the subject is a pronoun which immediately follows its referent, as in . . . <u>an attitude that will not brook . . .</u> (no. 9) note both of them.

8. From the organised lists that you have made, what can you deduce about the characteristics of the people and things that are subjects of <u>brook</u>?

9. Summarise your findings about the unit of meaning that has <u>brook</u> (verb) as its core, giving information about the effect it has on its cotext.

Datafile 06_brook.doc

1	again shown its determination not to	brook	any challenge to its authority. It
2	another indication that SLORC cannot	brook	any objections or protests against
3	about the ANC, about its inability to	brook	any criticism or opposition. Like
4	authenticity? Anthea: It doesn't	brook	any messing around. There is no
5	President Assad will be in no mood to	brook	any more. Treachery, however
6	absolutely useless. We will not	brook	any decision by any court from
7	unenthusiastic for Delorism, will not	brook	Britain's petulant isolation from
8	become a state of mind that does not	brook	contradiction. Yet a few modest
9	armed with an attitude that will not	brook	defeat. The opening scene of the
10	the proud Cleopatra would not	brook	. Learning of his plans, she
11	for school. Mother and father would	brook	no more of Malcolm's (or Rose's)
12	enemies within Germany that he would	brook	no opposition. Calling upon his
13	Yitzhak Shamir has said Israel will	brook	no interference in the affairs of
14	has repeatedly said it will	brook	no interference in what it
15	Yitzhak Shamir has said Israel will	brook	no interference concerning the
16	minded determination of the Tigers to	brook	no opposition in the Tamil areas of
17	do it at once. She would	brook	no argument or opposition and on
18	a leap. But Fisher's determination to	brook	no opposition meant that defective
19	needs or wants. Artemis-type women	brook	no nonsense from their menfolk, as
20	and those influenced by its rays will	brook	no denial in seizing their
21	and intolerant teachers, as they will	brook	no mispronunciation or mis-accent,
22	anger in her companion's veins would	brook	no control, and Sarah Ellis had
23	thin enough to make it clear they'd	brook	no interference, and his jaw was
24	Warn them that, on this one, we'll	brook	no interference. And if, by some
25	had an urgent appointment which would	brook	no delay. Ilara
26	of action for herself, one that would	brook	no interference. Pallas and Hart
27	laughter. Meanwhile, Eritrea's rulers	brook	no interference from their de jure
28	Francois Mitterrand, vowing to	brook	no interference from France's
29	or what have you) and they will	brook	no delay. This feat has never
30	of the country. And the army will	brook	no weakening of its power. In 1988,
31	fantastic. They fear no mocking, they	brook	no brickbats and from the moment
32	insistent about the tasks that will	brook	no delay but there is a need for
33	summer, and made clear that he would	brook	no dissent from the ERM line.
34	it was a sovereign state, and would	brook	no interference in its internal
35	a pistol, and Epstein himself would	brook	no opposition. He once ordered
36	avoid the terrifying Hackman who will	brook	no vigilantes in his town and
37	Department. The Constitution does not	brook	riddles, solved or unsolved.
38	that society would not always	brook	such nonsense. They had only to
39	out – that Mrs. Thatcher would not	brook	the thought of a husband and wife

Task 6

Key

1. no   26
   any   6

<u>Any</u> is often part of a negative construction.

2.

No.	Negative
1	not . . . any
2	cannot . . . any
3	inability . . . any
4	doesn't . . . any
5	no . . . any
6	not . . . any
7–10	not
11–36	no
37–39	not

From this evidence it can be assumed that <u>brook</u> characteristically occurs with a negative; in most cases this is <u>no</u> or <u>not</u>, but there is one instance (no. 3) of a lexical negative, where the negative is in the form of a prefix within a word. Since the concordance contains all the evidence of the word from a large corpus, and not a single instance occurs without a negative, it is fairly safe to assume that a positive use of <u>brook</u> would be an exceptionally unusual event.

3. would   9
   will   9
   to   3

The most common word class is the modal verb, with <u>will</u> and <u>would</u> as strong collocates. The form <u>'d</u> is most probably a shortened form of <u>would</u> and the form <u>'ll</u> is most probably a shortened form of <u>will</u>, so we can add these in to make ten of each type, and twenty modals in all.

4. The three instances which have <u>to</u> at N − 1 have a lexical anticipation of modality as follows:

- Number 18 – <u>determination</u> – a word indicating the sort of stubbornness that we hear in <u>would not</u>
- Number 28 – <u>vowing</u> – another, similar lexicalisation
- Number 16 – <u>determination</u> – again

The instances which do not have <u>no</u> at N+1 have modals as follows:

No.	Form	Notes
1	determination	lexicalised modality
2	cannot	modal
3	inability	lexicalised modality
4	doesn't	auxiliary
5	in no mood to	lexicalised modality
6	will	modal
7	will	modal
8	does	auxiliary
9	will	modal
10	would	modal
37	does	auxiliary
38	would	modal
39	would	modal

This leaves only six instances which have no expression of modality: the three with the auxiliary <u>does</u>, and nos. 20, 27 and 31. Of these the first five express generalisations, and the last is an odd phrase altogether. From this evidence we can safely say that the vast majority of instances of <u>brook</u> occur with a modal verb, usually of the <u>will</u>, <u>would</u> type but also occasionally of the <u>can</u> type. It is important to note, however, that in several instances the modal choice is LEXICALISED, and there is no grammatical choice of modal.

5. interference	9
opposition	4
delay	3

There is a lot of common meaning between <u>interference</u> and <u>opposition</u>; <u>delay</u> is a little different, but in the context of actions that frustrate the implementation of a plan, delay is a kind of inaction that has the same effect; and of course some delays are deliberately caused. To these we can add <u>challenge</u>, <u>objections</u>, <u>criticism</u>, <u>argument</u>, <u>nonsense</u>, <u>denial</u> and <u>dissent</u>. The next step is to look at the specific instances and see if the noun at N−2 can be interpreted in a similar way, if only in the particular line. For example, in no. 4, <u>messing around</u> probably refers to some action that is getting in the way of someone's plans; <u>decision</u> (no. 6) is neutral in itself, but the cotext probably goes on to specify a decision that would thwart a plan of action; <u>mispronunciation</u> in the context of <u>intolerant teachers</u> is clearly frustrating. The use of <u>control</u> in no. 22 has this kind of meaning also because the subject concerns an overwhelming anger; <u>vigilantes</u> (no. 36) joins the group with reference to someone whose behaviour is beyond the law; <u>weakening</u> (no. 30) means "being weakened" and refers back to <u>the army</u> as the organisation under threat of being weakened.

We are left with brickbats in no. 31, which is already a strange instance, and two instances of more in nos. 5 (any more) and 11 (more of . . .). In no. 5 the phrase refers back to something that has already been expressed, and since the following word, in a new sentence, is Treachery, we can get some idea of what any more refers to – something likely to fit into the list we are compiling. In line 11 the behaviour that is objected to has not yet been expressed, but it looks as if Malcolm is a child who has driven his parents to the end of their patience.

We have now associated together all the noun objects of the sentences that have no or any at N+1. The association is semantic, in that we claim a similarity of meaning; in some cases, particularly the repeated ones, the semantic strand is inherent in the word – that is to say, it will most likely be part of a dictionary definition of the word as in interference, but in many cases it is only when the word is interpreted in the specific instance that it acquires this meaning, and it would be most inappropriate for a dictionary to suggest that this meaning was inherent. For example, mispronunciation is a fault and the word is pejorative, but it does not normally mean a challenge to authority – only when the authorities are intolerant teachers of pronunciation is this meaning created by the text as a whole.

The local, temporary creation of meaning in a text is called REVERSAL, because our normal model for the creation of meaning is that it is brought to the text by the words; in cases of reversal the direction changes, and the text brings new meaning to the words – but only for a single instance.

6. Words following or: protests, opposition (twice), mis-accent. The first two have an inherent meaning that is appropriate to this set, but the third requires the cotext.

Number 8 (contradiction) also has an inherently appropriate meaning. Defeat, riddles and nonsense need to be focused in order to be seen as thwarting somone's plans, so for example defeat fits in when it is the subject of the clause who is in danger of being defeated. (Britain's petulant) isolation has to be understood in a particular political context; the word isolation only fits in with this meaning where someone is pressing for integration. Finally, (the) thought (of) . . . recalls the structure of no. 11, where whatever is causing offence has yet to come, and is not expressed in the short quotation that we have.

Clearly the semantic framework provided by brook has a powerful effect on the words around it; in this case it obliges its objects to include a particular strand of meaning; either an object noun is selected that already fits the prescription, or a noun is selected that can be interpreted as fitting the prescription, or the required meaning is projected onto the noun for this instance only.

7. The most repeated subject noun is determination, which occurs three times and shows once again the close relationship between the choice of the verb brook and the choice of modality, particularly in the sense of stubbornness. Related to determination are anger . . . , inability, (state of mind) and (attitude). (Nouns referred to by pronouns are in brackets.)

The only other repeated words are pronouns: the personal pronouns they (2), it (2) and we (2), he, she, one . . . , demonstrative those . . . and relatives which, that and who.

Among the singletons we find some loose groupings: "institutions" like SLORC, (the ANC), Israel, rulers, army, society, Constitution, state and (teachers); "people" like Assad, Cleopatra, Mitterrand (?), Epstein, (Hackman) and Mrs Thatcher; also mother and father and women.

There are two left over – (appointment), which suggests that the appointment is with a person likely not to brook delay, and (tasks) which get their urgency from someone's pressure. In no. 7 the subject noun is not present.

8. The prevailing impression of the collection of people and institutions that are represented in the subject position is one of figures of authority and centres of power. Nations and heads of nations include some hint of the autocratic – for example, the named women are Cleopatra and Mrs Thatcher, the unnamed are Artemis-type women and mother.

There is a curious absence of the pronouns I and you; the instances of we refer to spokespeople for nations or groups. It appears that people do not use this verb of their own personal behaviour, but ascribe it to others – their superiors in the case of spokespeople, and indomitable personalities by those who come up against them or observe their behaviour.

9. The core of the unit of meaning is the co-selection of brook and a negative – one of many possible kinds of negative but typically the emphatic variety where the word no follows a positive verb. Hypothetically, brook is almost a synonym of "tolerate", and in all the instances here it can be substituted without much change of meaning; what is lost is the fact that brook entails the negative and so is much more forceful.

Another element of the meaning is the attitude of the person who is the subject of the verb brook. This comes out in most instances in a modal verb, particularly would or will, but also in words like determination. Some of the people and institutions named as subjects lend support to this element of the meaning, since they are the kind of people or institutions that tend to be authoritarian.

People do not often say "I will not brook . . ." or "You wouldn't brook . . ." – in other words they do not say it of themselves or ascribe it to others face-to-face. It is much more common for them to have that said about them, because the phrase with brook has a pejorative meaning also; it is not nice not to brook things – perhaps the person is impatient or even arrogant.

There is a common element in the meaning of most of the objects of the clause with brook as verb. They can almost all be interpreted as some action or inaction that gets in the way of the implementation of a plan, and irritates the person in authority.

So you use brook when you want to say disparagingly of a person in authority that they cannot tolerate any manoeuvres against them, whether intentional or not. This meaning is a lot more specialised than just "tolerate".

Task 7

Subtle distinctions

Everyone knows, in a way, what IDIOMS are, but it is very difficult to define them. There is something quite specific and local about their meaning. The most popular definition of an idiom is that it is a phrase that has a meaning that cannot be predicted from the individual meanings of the words that make it up.

Idioms that are often quoted to illustrate this unique kind of meaning are, for example, <u>kick the bucket</u>, <u>red herring</u> and <u>it's raining cats and dogs</u>. These mean, respectively, to die, an irrelevant diversion, and it's raining very heavily. Although some of the words keep their normal meaning, e.g. <u>raining</u>, it is not possible to guess the meaning of the phrase as a whole.

There are examples of this kind of idiom in Section 4. But there are also idiomatic phrases made up of words that do not change in meaning. As well as its *literal* meaning, such a phrase is used in a special sense without any change in the meanings of the words in the phrase.

In this task we will study one of these idioms, based around the collocation <u>best thing</u>.

1. Study the concordance sample of <u>best thing</u> (datafile **07_bestthing.doc**). Look at the words immediately to the left of <u>best</u> (position N−1) and find the most frequent form; then do the same calculation at the position N+1, the word immediately to the right of <u>thing</u>. Of the two, select the most frequent. This gives us, as a starting point, the strongest word-pattern in the immediate environment of <u>best thing</u>. (For an explanation of the position notation, see the Glossary under SPAN.)

2. Of those lines that have a different choice at N−1, look for this frequent word at N−2. How many are there? List the words that come in between. Which lines are left over?

3. Now look at the right-hand side, the words that come immediately after <u>best thing</u>. The commonest word can be either a preposition or the marker of the infinitive. Classify the seven instances here into one or the other.

4. What other words occur at N−1 more than once? Of the words that occur only once, which share the word class of one of the repeated words? Which lines are now left over?

5. Now look on the right-hand side for the first verb. Stop when you come to the end of a sentence. Make a list of the verbs.

6. Consider the lines containing the commonest verb. Is there another verb just afterwards? What is it? Note the grammar at this point.

7. Now we are going to look for what best thing refers to. It must be somewhere in the text, because "best things" do not exist in the world in the same way that chairs and tables do. Start with the seven instances analysed above, where the phrase is part of the subject of is/was. Is the "best thing" to be found just afterwards, in the complement of the clause?

8. Look through the other lines and see if there are any more where the referent of best thing is in the complement of the clause. If you find it, note where it is; if it is not present make a guess as to where it is likely to be.

9. In those cases where the referent is to the right, which of the referents start with infinitives? Do these have the verb is/was just in front of them? Is it possible to add to do between best thing and is/was? If so, how do these structures compare with the diagram in §6?

10. Check through the lines where the referent is at N−1. How often is it the case that the referent is the subject of a clause with the verb "be" and the best thing is complement? At the same time note how many referents are themselves, or include, words of reference, passing the reader on to a previous referent.

11. We have divided the lines according to where the referent for best thing is, which depends largely on whether that phrase is subject or complement of a "to be" clause. Now consider if there is any difference in meaning between the two uses of the phrase.

Datafile 07_bestthing.doc

1	or me, this gumbo is the next best	thing	to a trip to New Orleans. Tender
2	else I would've done. It was the best	thing	for shareholders. It was the right
3	people are beyond help. Now the best	thing	you can do is to help us.' I
4	else. And that, ok that was the best	thing	that was available at the time but
5	not sure that's necessarily the best	thing	," he said quickly. But
6	they knew on instinct that the best	thing	to do was to push, to take the
7	as if his mind had shut down. Best	thing	for him, to be pissed and not be
8	and cry. 'I thought it was the best	thing	that was ever likely to happen to
9	What's happened is much the best	thing	. Father and Aunt Ginny will have a
10	and therefore I thought the best	thing	was to stamp upon it at once,
11	of study surely, the very best	thing	he can do is devote his spare time
12	with myself. So I thought the best	thing	I could do was come along here and
13	and done, Tis still the best	thing	under the sun. On Malted
14	react and I decided that the best	thing	to do would be to move up to them
15	a series of issues here and the best	thing	is to separate them out into a
16	with me would have been the best	thing	ever to happen to Gavin. I just
17	All Played Out was easily the best	thing	to come out of Italia '90) goes to
18	assigning blame becomes the next best	thing	. On health care, Missouri
19	And I'm not sure what the best	thing	to do would have been. And it's
20	you know I don't know what the best	thing	is to do. It's been g+ you know it'
21	say anything clever. In fact the best	thing	to do is just sit and let them
22	Englishman (Hugh Grant, the best	thing	in the film) is button-holed by a
23	of doom and gloom this is the best	thing	we could have had." As the
24	Christine, 43, said: 'It's best	thing	that ever happened to us. It made
25	in Albertville, the next best	thing	is to be in your own living room
26	saying: 'Craig said it was the best	thing	he had ever done to turn pro. I am
27	mixture of fuel and air to make the	thing	explode. The best method of
28	this. [tuts] Right. Well the	thing	I think the best thing to do is for
29	was a change of direction. I felt the	thing	I could do best and not many other
30	and I described the whole	thing	as best I could and they looked at
31	This is the most wonderful	thing	. This is the best thing you've ever
32	Imbert. Q: What's the best/worst	thing	to do if you think someone is
33	No answer. 12% 39 Do you	thing	the best things in life are free?

Task 7

Key

1. N−1   <u>the</u>   20
   N+1   <u>to</u>   6

2. N−2   <u>the</u>   4
   Words in between: <u>next</u> 3, <u>very</u> (i.e. <u>the next best thing</u>, etc.)
   Lines where <u>the</u> is at neither N−1 nor N−2: nos. 7 and 24 only

3. <u>To</u> is a preposition in the first line only; otherwise it is the infinitive marker in six cases.

4. Repeated words at N−1: <u>he</u> 3, <u>is</u> 3, <u>that</u> 3, <u>for</u> 2.

Singletons

pronouns (like <u>he</u>): <u>I</u>, <u>we</u>, <u>you</u>   total with <u>he</u> = 6
prepositions (like <u>for</u>): <u>on</u>, <u>in</u>, <u>under</u>, <u>to</u>   total with <u>for</u> = 6
verb "be" (like <u>is</u>): <u>was</u>   total with <u>is</u> = 4

How many are left? The three word classes above add up to 16; with <u>that</u> (× 3) and <u>to</u> (× 6) as an infinitive marker, the total is 25 out of 26; only no. 10, where the word at N−1 is <u>Father</u>, is left; this word begins a new sentence and so is probably an unrelated choice.

5. <u>do</u> 8   (also <u>done</u>)
   <u>was</u> 2   (also <u>be</u>)
   also   happen, happened

6. Verbs that immediately follow <u>do</u>: <u>is</u> 3, <u>was</u> 2, <u>would be</u>, <u>would have been</u>. All these are forms of the verb "be"; in one line <u>do</u> ends the sentence.
   The grammar shows that between <u>best thing</u> and the verb "be" is a clause or phrase containing the word <u>do</u>. This can be seen in a simple diagram:

		to		
the best thing	you		can	do
	he			
	I		could	

All this structure is the subject of the verb "be", which follows.

7. In six cases – nos. 4, 11, 12, 14, 19 and 21 – the referent is the complement. However, in no. 19 there is a complication because <u>best thing</u> is in a relative clause introduced by <u>what</u>. This word is the grammatical complement of <u>would have been</u>, and the referent of <u>best thing</u>; such a word would normally follow the verb, but since it is a relative pronoun it must come first in the clause.

With this in mind we can now add no. 20 to the group; it is almost the same as 19 but has an extra change in word order so that the verb <u>is</u> precedes <u>do</u>; there is no difference in the grammatical relations.

8.
- In nos. 10, 15, 25 and 26 the referent is to the right.
- In nos. 1, 2, 4, 5, 8, 9, 13, 17, 22, 23 and 24 the referent is to the left.
- In nos. 7 and 16 there is no clear referent; I guess it is to the left.

9.

Line	Infinitive?	<u>to do?</u>
10	yes	yes
15	yes	yes
25	yes	no
26	yes	no

Numbers 10 and 15 fit into the diagram, which can be expanded to:

the best thing		to		do	is	to INFINITIVE
	you		can			
	he				was	
	I		could			

In no. 25 <u>to do</u> would clash in meaning with <u>to be</u> so it cannot be introduced; but this clash points up the ironical meaning – being in a place is not an action.

Number 26 is superficially similar to no. 11, for instance, but there is one important difference: <u>the best thing</u> is the complement in 26, and <u>to turn pro</u> is anticipated by <u>it</u>, which is the subject. In no. 11, and all the other lines with <u>do</u> and the infinitives, the syntax is the other way round.

10. Numbers 1, 2, 4, 5, 8, 13 and 23 answer "yes" to all these queries; the referent is the subject and itself makes a further reference back; the verb is a form of "be".

In nos. 17 and 18, and probably 16, the referent is expressed as subject in the clause and there is no further reference chain: in no. 17 this is <u>All Played Out</u>, in 18 <u>assigning blame</u>, and in 16 <u>. . . with me</u> (no. 18 has <u>becomes</u> as a verb which is similar to "be" in this context). In no. 9 the verb is <u>happened</u>, and the relative pronoun <u>what</u> affects the word order as we saw above in relation to nos. 19 and 20, but the referent is clearly on the left-hand side.

Number 7 needs to be interpreted because it is very colloquial; if it is interpreted as "the best thing for him is to be pissed" then it is very similar to no. 25, and is ironical – perhaps by being drunk he does not experience fully something unpleasant. If this reading is accepted then no. 7 joins those that fit into the diagram at §9.

11. When <u>(the) best thing</u> has a backward referent, it is unrestricted in meaning, and means "the best possible event". When it has a forward referent is occurs just after some unfortunate event has been described, and it means "the least damaging action in the circumstances". The is called "damage limitation" (Tognini Bonelli, 1992). The two meanings are substantially different – one is a very desirable event, and the other is an action which is seen as the least unpleasant of a set of alternatives.

So the phrase can be deployed in two different ways to make two different meanings, without the meanings of the words changing in any dramatic way.

Task 8

Meaning flavour

Words influence each other, pass judgements on each other, and lay down guidelines for each other's interpretation. One word can prepare the reader or listener to receive another one that comes just a little later, and to understand it in a certain way. The interconnections among words that occur close to each other are so intricate that quite often we are sure that they are not independently chosen, but COSELECTED.

1. This section explores the coselection of words by asking a question to begin with: What sort of things do you incur? Study the file **08_incur.doc** and look at the words that immediately follow <u>incur</u>. It is most likely that the object of the verb <u>incur</u> will come immediately after it; locate the HEADWORD and classify the objects according to (a) the meaning of the headword, and (b) the determiners that precede the headword. Note other modifiers and qualifiers that surround the headword.

2. Look at the adjectives and see if any support the gloomy outlook of the nouns, or otherwise. Look at the noun modifiers of the headwords, and the words in the prepositional phrases, and more widely in the instances, and see finally if any of them escape this orientation to gloominess.

3. Now look at the words that precede <u>incur</u>. Take into account up to three words to the left, and look for other verb elements, adverbials and conjunctions that affect the timing and modality of the verb. Remember that this form, the BASE or uninflected form of the verb, has three main syntactic functions – simple present tense, imperative, and infinitive (following "to" or following a modal verb).

4. What kind of meaning goes with the selection of the "to" infinitive? Summarise the verb cotext of <u>incur</u>.

5. What kind of person or thing incurs these financial and other liabilities? Unfortunately the instances are often too short for the subject of the verb <u>incur</u> to be identified, but in those instances where it is clear, note it and classify the list you build up.

Datafile 08_incur.doc

1	worth between YEN 250m and YEN 500m	incur	a tax rate of 65%. A sum
2	and that the confession may also	incur	a torrent of moral judgment.
3	of 40m. Punch would also	incur	an additional capital gains tax
4	don't run a single minute late and	incur	costly overtime payments. Pavarotti
5	that a sentient entity can	incur	a loss. For a critical discussion
6	today have product liability and can	incur	legal damages if they place a
7	or so. I know if I cash my super in I	incur	a hefty tax bill. Is it possible to
8	perceived as negative that may	incur	bad publicity. It is surely time
9	Allen said: 'No one state should	incur	sanctions when making a stand
10	Countreys, lest otherwise he should	incur	great danger and loss in the
11	must be invested overseas, or if they	incur	unusually large costs to get their
12	face deduction of 10 points if they	incur	that grading in 1996. Cricket:
13	APPLE COMPUTER expects to	incur	a $700 million loss in the
14	The restructuring is expected to	incur	a one-off charge of less than
15	The company said it continued to	incur	an operating loss due to increased
16	of fiscal 1990 and we are likely to	incur	additional restructuring charges as
17	path and it does not expect to	incur	any abnormal restructuring costs in
18	Mm. That means that we have to	incur	that expenditure. And equally I
19	are many overheads we are forced to	incur	in order to make our judgements as
20	round on Everest Fol Amour only to	incur	three quarters of a time fault.
21	and for any losses or costs we	incur	as a result of any breach by you of
22	trading markets. American firms will	incur	short-run adjustment costs but
23	not to be called in as they would	incur	penalty rates, 'after all it's only
24	the gospel and reform sinners would '	incur	the highest displeasure of his
25	was open to competitive tender would	incur	costs. But Mr Wakeham emphasised
26	Western Front. Attacking armies would	incur	huge losses for gains that could
27	to seek a method which would	incur	the lowest loss of life and the
28	order to place the shares and would	incur	advisory and other costs. The
29	OF POCKET EXPENSES: If you	incur	out of pocket expenses, notify the
30	card. You can relax, knowing that you	incur	no liability for fraudulent

Task 8

Key

1.

No.	Headword	Type	Det.	Adj.	Noun	Prep. phrase
1	rate	money	a		X[a]	X
2	torrent[c]	morals	a			X
3	tax	money	an	X	XX	
4	payments	money		X	X	
5	loss	money	a			
6	damages	money		X		
7	bill	money	a	X		
8	publicity	publicity		X		
9	sanctions	politics				
10	danger	trade		X		
11	costs	money		Xm[b]		
12	grading	sport	that			
13	loss	money	a	X		
14	charge	money	a	X		X
15	loss	money	an		X	
16	charges	money		X	X	
17	costs	money	any	X	X	
18	expenditure	money	that			
19[d]	overheads	money	any			
20	fault	sport	a	−[e]	X	
21[f]	losses or costs	money	any			
22	costs	money			XX	
23	rates	money			X	
24	displeasures	morals	the	X		X
25	costs	money				
26	losses	warfare		X		
27	loss	warfare	the	X		X
28	costs	money		XX		
29	expenses	money			X	
30	liability	money	no			X

[a] "X" in a column indicates that the object includes such an element of structure.
[b] "m" in the "Adj." column means that the adjective is itself modified by an adverb of degree such as "very".
[c] This analysis follows conventional lines, but there is a sound argument in noun groups of the quantifying type for considering the second noun as the main headword. In this instance judgement would be the headword, and the type classification is based on that. Note also that judgement in this sense is an uncountable noun. See Sinclair (1991), Chapter 6.
[d] In this instance the main verb is passive and so it is the subject of that verb that is analysed in the table.
[e] This instance is of a clear quantifier, three quarters of, which does not have headword status.
[f] In this instance incur is in a relative clause, and the relevant noun group is in the main clause just before incur.

Comments

Most of the headwords concern money (21 out of 30, 70%), and of the rest two concern morals, two sport and two warfare, leaving publicity, politics and trade with one each. The commonest nouns are <u>loss(es)</u> and <u>costs</u> (six of each), and many of the others emphasise the flow of resources away (ten). In all 22 of the headwords are of this kind.

The determiners are mainly indefinite – <u>a</u>, <u>an</u>, <u>any</u>, <u>no</u>, totalling 12. To these must be added instances where the headword is plural (12) or uncountable (2), bringing the total to 26 (87%). This tells us that <u>incur</u> introduces new information in the object.

2.
- Gloomy adjectives: <u>costly</u>, <u>hefty</u>, <u>bad</u>, <u>abnormal</u> (4).
- Intensifying a gloomy headword: <u>additional</u>, <u>great</u>, <u>unusually large</u>, <u>$700 million</u>, <u>additional</u>, <u>highest</u>, <u>huge</u> (7).
- Total adjectives supporting gloom: 11 out of 14 – almost 80%.
- Noun modifiers number eleven. Most are descriptive, and only two are gloomy: <u>tax</u> and <u>penalty</u>.
- Elsewhere we note <u>liability</u> (6), <u>negative</u> (8), <u>deduction</u> (12), <u>forced to</u> (19), <u>breach</u> (21) and <u>fraudulent</u> (30).

Summary

The orientation of unhappiness concerning resources, primarily financial resources, slipping away is expressed in the headwords and the adjectives that modify them. Not a single instance escapes this orientation. We can thus say that the verb <u>incur</u> sets up an expectation of gloom, and we expect to find that its object expresses a loss of something important. You do not incur rewards or prizes, but penalties or charges against you.

3.

No.	Type	Modal	To-infinitive	Other words
1	present			
2	infinitive	may		also
3	infinitive	would		also
4	infinitive	don't		
5	infinitive	can		
6	infinitive	can		
7	present			if
8	infinitive	may		
9	infinitive	should		
10	infinitive	should		
11	present			if
12	present			if

No.	Type	Modal	To-infinitive	Other words
13	infinitive		expects to	
14	infinitive		is expected to	
15	infinitive		continued to	
16	infinitive		are likely to	
17	infinitive		does not expect to	
18	infinitive		have to	
19	infinitive		are forced to	
20	infinitive		only to	
21	present			any (2)
22	infinitive	will		
23	infinitive	would		
24	infinitive	would		
25	infinitive	would		
26	infinitive	would		
27	infinitive	would		
28	infinitive	would		
29	present			if
30	present			that, no

Comments

There are no imperatives, and very few simple present tense instances. The majority (15) follow modals, and the next largest group (8) are instances of the "to" infinitive. (Actually no. 18 is often classed as a modal.)

There are seven instances of the simple present tense; of these four are in conditional ("if") clauses, where modals hardly ever occur. Two others (nos. 21 and 30) are in subordinate clauses, and the only single instance of a simple present tense in a main clause is no. 1.

4. Most of the "to" infinitives concern the likely future; two concern obligation. In general the cotexts are modals, particularly <u>would</u>, and "to" infinitives, with simple present tenses in subordinate clauses, especially "if" clauses. This, combined with the damaging nature of the typical things that people incur, suggests an overall semantic prosody of threat or warning.

5.

No.	Subject	Type
2	the confession	person
3	Punch	institution
5	a sentient entity	person
7	I	person
9	no one state	institution

No.	Subject	Type
10	he	person
11	they	institution
12	they	institution
13	APPLE COMPUTER	institution
14	the restructuring	institution
15	the company	institution
16	we	institution
17	it	institution
18	we	institution
19	we	institution
21	we	person
22	American firms	institution
23	they	institution
24	the gospel and reform sinners	people
26	attacking armies	institution
27	(a method) which	institution
29	you	person
30	you	person

Comment

In sixteen instances it is an institution, a company, a state or an army that incurs a liability, loss or penalty. In the remaining eight of those whose subject can be discerned, it is a person or people; these people incur things in relation to an institution, because to incur something is a sociolegal consequence of one's actions, and not an interpersonal relationship.

Task 9

Extensions of grammar

Grammar is usually described separately from lexis. There is rarely any reference to lexical matters in a grammar because grammarians feel that grammar explains the powerful general rules of the language, while lexis just deals with the detailed meaning of individual words and phrases. Recently, though, the notion of "lexicogrammar" has come into some advanced grammars and made them a little sensitive to lexis.

There are, however, places in a grammar where the generalisations do not apply, when the "rules" can be "broken", and the only way to describe these places is by using the lexical choices. As an example of this, let us review the rule for an adjective standing in for a noun. In English it is not correct to say "Send your complaints to the responsible", though – unlike the example above – the meaning is clear; the sentence translates easily into French or German, and a similar sentence, "Give your spare cash to the poor", is acceptable. How do grammars explain this feature?

Unfortunately, they usually do not explain why some adjectives can be used in this structure and some cannot, or even list those that can. Nor do they suggest any principle by which we could guess at the normal usage.[1] They just give a few examples and/or a short list of words that probably occur. However, looking at the lists provided there does seem to be some SEMANTIC PREFERENCE; here is one such list:[2]

> the lazy, the lame, the fat, the indifferent, the leaning, the halt, the rich, the poor, the unemployed, the elderly, the young, the transient

1. Do you detect a strand of meaning that is common to most of the words in this list? How would you express it? Are there any clear exceptions, or any words which can occur with this meaning but do not always? If any do not seem to belong to this list, check with a dictionary that they do not have a minor or old-fashioned meaning that is relevant. Consult the datafiles **09_rich.doc** and **09_halt.doc** for some instances of <u>the rich</u> and <u>the halt</u> that may be helpful.

---

[1] There are some honourable and recent exceptions; *The Longman Grammar of Spoken and Written English* (1999) is not exhaustive, but it does quote actual instances. The *Cobuild English Grammar* (1990) does the same, and the *Cobuild Pattern Grammar* (1998) lists all the relevant adjectives and classifies them as to their meanings. See the References in the Preface.

[2] *The Longman Grammar*, page 520, excluding nationality adjectives (<u>the Welsh</u>) and those that refer to events (<u>the unlikely</u>).

2. Now consult the datafile **09_borderson.doc**. This concordance was made by selecting arithmetically 35 instances of borders on. Look at the phrases immediately to the right of on, and classify them with reference to both the lexis and the grammar.

3. From now on we will ignore the geographical references of border. Examine the remaining phrases and list the nouns and adjectives that are the headwords. What kinds of words are they? Do they share any semantic features? Are there systematic semantic differences between the nouns and the adjectives? Note any exceptions or marginal cases.

4. The phrase that we started with has borders on and not "border on", which is the normal form in which we access a verb. So we will now investigate whether the other forms of the LEMMA "border" combine with on in the same way as we have observed. For this see the datafile **09_lemma.doc**, which contains 20 instances of the other forms of the lemma – border, bordering and bordered.

5. Summarise what has emerged about this phrase, in particular how the structure of the phrase creates meaning and what conclusions are indicated for lexicogrammar.

6. One final examination of the concordances. We do not know the precise extent of the influence of this pattern. For example, the phrase borders on is comparative, and so there is likely to be a systematic semantic relationship between the subject element and the object element. We have been concentrating on the object in this study, and have not even glanced at the language in front of the phrase, so now let us have another quick look at the datafile **09_borderson.doc**. In one or two instances the left-hand cotext is not long enough to show the whole subject, but where there is a clear subject phrase compare it with the object to see what sort of relationship they have. Guess a little if necessary.

Consider the construction of the subject group as well as its meaning. Make a judgement about whether the subject and object make a clear comparative relationship (whether relative or absolute) naturally, by their own meaning, or whether it is their position in this structure that makes you think of how they can be related.

Datafile 09_rich.doc

1   Police last night feared the bomber could be targeting the rich and famous.

2   For most people this means returning next year. For the rich it means renting a villa; for the seriously rich, building one

3   excluding food from a goods and services tax would be a bonanza for the rich . I had not realised that the rich ate so

4   Connecticut, which brags that it was founded 'of, by, and for the rich ', to the tiny Bank of San Francisco

5   the scholarships with private 'add-on' funds. 18 That might prevent the rich from immediately setting up exclusive elementary schools charging

6   were told also to send food and drink to the poor. In this way the rich could atone for their largesse and hope to placate the envy of the

7   And he wouldn't have just stolen from the rich to give to the poor. He'd have robbed them, kicked their heads in and

8   issue holding up an agreement. They say the measure benefits only the rich , and if they go along with

9   attack on the rich and powerful. Wofford: For 10 years, the rich have gotten richer at the same time the vast majority of working

10   class tax cut and now we've got big tax increases. Sure, more for the rich , but the tax increases apply to every income level.

11   desire to realize the popular will or serve the narrow interests of the rich , but rather a matter of the imperatives of the system being exerted

12   the layout of British towns and cities – was one of the reasons why the rich should recognise that growing inequality and social fragmentation could

13   Keats was a republican, inspired by an enduring contempt for the rich By PAUL FOOT IN TWO days last week, a few hundred yards

14   from their homes, in part because of the subsidised luxuries of the rich . The local impact of air travel is scarcely less severe.

15   though, some of O'Rourke's jokes look a little narrow-minded. In Eat the Rich , he admits he has nothing new to say about capitalism or socialism, and

Datafile 09_halt.doc

1	attention was being paid to the	halt	and the lame – among them Sir Julian
2	I, a sardonic retelling of the	halt	and the blind helping one another.
3	for this particular group of the	halt	and the lame. Science and
4	they come, the limp, the lame and the	halt	, all of them drawn from the rent-a-
5	So, too, was the shunning of the	halt	and the lame and the dying. That was
6	here, ministering to the lame and the	halt	." They haven't given you your
7	expect nunneries to be full of the	halt	, the lame, the sick and the
8	get him moving too, he thought, the	halt	, the blind and the deaf, got to get
9	procession of the lame, the	halt	and the blind, some with arms in
10	left everyone in place – the old, the	halt	, the lame and the blind. Yet at the
11	disciples, even the lame and the	halt	, came in their great multitudes up
12	entire wasp population, the sick, the	halt	, the fuzzy, to enjoy her. A single-
13	of their costly collection of the	halt	, lame and suspended. Rugby
14	trend, 'we may end up getting the	halt	and the lame.'

Datafile 09_borderson.doc

1	and on mutual respect for existing	borders"	on 16 December, Karimov became
2	is more than just a way of life – it	borders	on a religion. But there is
3	of the laws of the sea sometimes	borders	on arrogance. Not only should the
4	international collaboration is great and	borders	on cartel-like behaviour.
5	who say using the extremist label	borders	on demagoguery and will only serve
6	Yugoslavia. What is occurring there	borders	on genocide. No country or society
7	Careless but losing two in the one day	borders	on incompetence. Now Charlie
8	Turkey, the only NATO country which	borders	on Iraq, is playing a key role in
9	Her mastery of the short story	borders	on perfection. kate saunders
10	country's stagnant growth, which now	borders	on recession. Here again, the
11	challenge looms ugly when recession	borders	on slump. Everybody is on edge,
12	The author, a lifelong fan,	borders	on the obsessive. He portrays
13	has a streak of bravery which	borders	on the foolish. She has delicate
14	to buy. A family with three children	borders	on the socially acceptable, four
15	even harbour a passion for DIY that	borders	on the obsessive. But there is
16	the Sierra Madre" as he dubs them)	borders	on the eccentric. Mountain lions
17	courses and opportunities, that it	borders	on the embarrassing. This
18	the straight, but his winning effort	borders	on the sensational because the
19	amount of work he is required to do	borders	on the incredible. In the case of
20	maxim 'The collector's passion	borders	on the chaos of memories.'
21	before staged protests at these two	borders	on the east and west of their
22	speaking to troops in Xinjian which	borders	on the Soviet Central Asian
23	clash. He said: 'The hostility there	borders	on the dangerous.' Black players
24	and – and to performing them sort of	borders	on the surreal. He had his own
25	most dangerous regions on Earth. It	borders	on the Serbian province of Kosovo,
26	a professional solicitousness which	borders	on the dangerous edge of
27	savings accounts versus shares,	borders	on the irresponsible.
28	an independent Bosnia in its pre-war	borders.	On the contrary, his private
29	His love for all things maritime	borders	on the obsessional. He is truly
30	Not surprisingly, the atmosphere	borders	on the surreal. Wander into the
31	The atmosphere of paranoia	borders	on the pathological. The sky, a
32	then Claire makes a statement that	borders	on the downright cocky. When I ask
33	The linear intensity of their songs	borders	on the paranoid and, although
34	and an easy-going demeanour which	borders	on the charismatic, it's hardly
35	popular music. In some cases, this	borders	on wholesale plagiarism. That's

Datafile 09_lemma.doc

1	250,000 home on the Essex–Suffolk	border on	the line because 'the action has
2	American currency.) Some attractions	border on	the absurd. Not to be outdone by
3	The women crossed the Albanian	border on	foot on Monday evening.
4	of Montenegro after crossing a river	border on	improvised rafts. The agency
5	attack the Barn owl territories that	border on	their woods, as Winger seems to
6	captured on the Macedonian	border on	March 31. The Red Cross
7	each side and can match up with the	border on	the wall.
8	middle-aged Peter Pans the effect	bordered on	the tragic. At first I thought
9	him a kind of power that sometimes	bordered on	the erotic. Tonight, as he
10	hundred-yard stretch of highway,	bordered on	either side by small
11	and their defensive effort	bordered on	the shameful, especially on the
12	Verdict: Rich and creamy but	bordering on	sickly. Flavours include:
13	as production designer. In an act	bordering on	the impertinent, he borrowed
14	warned that earlier letters were '	bordering on	intimidation of audit'. Such
15	their tufts and 'buns' in a state	bordering on	religious ecstasy. The fervor
16	I have ever seen. He was confident	bordering on	the brash and showed little
17	and were treated with a respect	bordering on	irony. They seldom appeared to
18	about media conspiracies. 'Distaste	bordering on	contempt' is just about right.
19	recognition in this country is	bordering on	a national shame. McRae's
20	know Goli to be a sound bidder, but	bordering on	the conservative. It was easy

Task 9

Key

1. These all refer to people, and most of them refer to people in an unfortunate condition. <u>Rich</u> is the only word that for most readers will have positive connotations, but a glance at the datafile makes it clear that <u>the rich</u> is almost always used in a context of insult, criticism or disparagement of rich people. That is to say, in the opinion of the authors and speakers whose usage is recorded, being rich has an unfortunate side, and that is the interpretation used when it is used as the headword of a group with the definite article in front of it.

<u>Elderly</u> and <u>young</u> may seem fairly neutral, but in this company it seems that they may indicate disadvantage. The principal collocates of <u>the elderly</u> are <u>care</u>, <u>children</u>, <u>disabled</u>, <u>women</u> and <u>help</u>. Needless to say, it is the perceived vulnerability of women and children that makes them prominent here.

<u>Halt</u> is not normally a quality associated with people, but there is an old meaning "lame", which occurs in the King James Bible of 1611; note from the datafile that it is not used on its own, and almost always nowadays it occurs with its synonym <u>lame</u>.

We can conclude from this that the meaning created by the structure

<u>the</u> + adj-headword

is of people who are characterised by a certain quality that marks them off as different from the majority of people, and leads to them being perceived as vulnerable and perhaps requiring social protection or open to social criticism.

2. Number 1 is a date, the only one. Number 2 is a noun phrase made of the indefinite article and an abstract noun, the only one. Numbers 3, 4, 5, 6, 7, 10, 11 and 35 are noun phrases made up of just an abstract noun, with no article. Number 8 is a place-name, and nos. 22 and 25 are also place-names, beginning with the definite article; no. 21 is a geographical reference. In no. 28 there is a sentence boundary between <u>borders</u> and <u>on</u>, and the <u>on-</u> phrase is <u>on the contrary</u>.

The remaining 19 instances are made up of <u>the</u> followed by an abstract expression. In nos. 20 and 26 it is a noun phrase, and in the others there is an adjective as headword; in two of these cases (nos. 14 and 32) the adjective is itself modified by an adverb.

From these observations it seems that the most prominent feature of these structures is the presence of an abstract adjective or noun in the HEADWORD position. A summary of our structural observations with respect to the abstract expressions is:

Article	Modifier	Headword	
definite	adjective		1
			1
indefinite	Ø	noun	1
	adjective		2
Ø	Ø		6
definite	adverb	adjective	2
	Ø		16

The numbers are conclusive – over 60% of the noun groups contain <u>the</u> and an adjective head, over a quarter have a noun head and no article, and the rest is minor variation.

3. <u>Nouns</u>
religion
arrogance
(cartel-like) behaviour
demagoguery
genocide
incompetence
perfection
recession
slump
chaos (of memories)
(dangerous) edge
(wholesale) plagiarism

<u>Adjectives</u>
obsessive
foolish
(socially) acceptable
obsessive
eccentric
embarrassing
sensational
incredible
dangerous
surreal
irresponsible
obsessional
surreal
pathological
(downright) cocky
paranoid
charismatic

These are mainly words of extreme mental states or character traits, mostly indicating mental disturbance or unacceptable behaviour. It is probably no accident that the repeated words in the list above are <u>obsessive/obsessional</u>, <u>surreal</u> and <u>dangerous</u>.

Cases for comment

- Number 2, <u>a religion</u>. The extreme meaning is relative here rather than absolute. Practising religion is important and serious for many people, and is not usually regarded as extreme behaviour (though fanaticism is a close relation); but if a person gives too much importance and commitment to some aspect of ordinary living then a comparison with religion exposes the lack of balance.
- Number 4, <u>cartel-like behaviour</u>. Cartels are regarded as unacceptable conspiracies in the prevailing economic conventions of the times.
- Number 9, <u>perfection</u>. This is a positive quality, and so contrasts with most of the instances. Perfection, however, is usually regarded as unattainable, so there may be a hint of irony when it is used in this way. The wider cotext shows that it is part of a very short – three line – review of a book, and this does sound like a rather extravagant compliment to pay in such a casual mention.
- Number 14, <u>the socially acceptable</u>. The context is that big families are unusual, and a maximum of two children is the norm. So I would have expected "socially unacceptable" here, and I can find no reason other than irony why this instance should run precisely contrary to the vast majority in the concordance. Perhaps the adverb <u>socially</u> obscures the way the structure normally specifies the meaning – without it the phrasing is very odd indeed.
- Number 32, <u>downright cocky</u>. Like no. 2, this is relative rather than absolute. <u>Cocky</u> is mildly disparaging in normal use, but hardly indicates the extreme margins of behaviour; <u>downright</u> pushes it towards the extreme.
- Number 34, <u>the charismatic</u>. Like no. 9, this is a word which indicates a person of unusual talents, but of a positive kind. Again the wider cotext suggests that the compliments are almost too extravagant to be true.

4. Based on this evidence, the form <u>border on</u> is more likely to refer to geographical borders than mental ones; only <u>the absurd</u> out of seven instances has abstract reference. The form <u>bordered</u> works in the other direction, and adds <u>the tragic,</u> <u>the erotic</u> and <u>the shameful</u> to the list compiled earlier. <u>Bordering</u> is the most numerous of the forms and has all objects but one of abstract reference; no. 12 is marginal, to do with flavours. The list of adjectives that occur in this construction now includes <u>the impertinent,</u> <u>the brash</u> and <u>the conservative</u> ("conservative" is to do with bidding at auctions, where the other extreme is presumably "rash", and "sound" lies in between). Other abstract noun groups are <u>religious ecstasy,</u> <u>irony,</u> <u>contempt</u> and <u>a national shame</u>.

The conclusion that we derive from this last datafile is that all of the forms of the lemma "border" with <u>on</u> can occur with the kind of abstract noun group that we have been studying, but the uninflected form, <u>border</u>, is the least likely, because of its common use to mean geographical or political borders.

5. To summarise, the construction consisting of the phrase <u>borders on</u> with an object which has as its head an abstract expression seems to make a very

powerful kind of meaning, and it makes its own local grammatical rules. There are a number of minor varieties of this structure, but the two main ones between them account for the vast majority of instances. These are an abstract noun without any article, and the definite article followed by a word that is normally regarded as an adjective. Most of these objects share an unusual meaning, of a mental state or a character trait which is considered abnormal or extreme. With borders on the whole expression serves to define an area that is on the limit of what is acceptable in ordinary life.

English has such few inflections and such a relaxed attitude to word class that we may ask why the adjectives keep their word class in such a structure; why do they not "become" nouns? This is indeed a possibility but it does not simplify the descriptive work, because we have seen that there are considerable limitations in general on the use of such words, which will have to be accounted for whatever word class we say they are. The words usually refer to people who have the named quality or attribute, and it makes them vulnerable.

With borders on, this vulnerability is further focused as set out above, and the same features are found, in varying amounts, in the other forms of the lemma "borders" occurring with on.

There are a small number of instances where the tight conventions of the local grammar are relaxed. If the phrase that follows borders on does not itself indicate a point just beyond the limit of rational and acceptable behaviour, then the structure exerts pressure on the words to carry that kind of meaning. If – as in the case of perfection and charismatic – this is not possible, then the phrase still carries the semantic marks of the pressure, and hints at irony.

In this small corner of lexicogrammar we have found a structure which is regarded as ungrammatical in most grammars but is here normal and regular. It refers to the character and behaviour of people in highly specific terms, and wherever possible imposes this meaning on the words that occur around it. This is so strong that in the instance (no. 14 above) which appears to be an exact counterexample, it is difficult to avoid the conclusion that it is ironical.

We do not as yet know if there are other phrases like borders on which attract similar lexicogrammatical patterns, or whether the set of nouns and adjectives that we have gathered in this study are to be found elsewhere in the lexicogrammar, realising other elements of structure. That is to say, we are not sure just how local this kind of pattern is. But its position in relation to a conventional general grammar is quite clear – it lies substantially outside the ability of the grammar to describe it.

6. In general the object elements refer to mental states which are beyond the limits of normality, and the subject elements may refer to related states which are within the range of normal behaviour. But there are some points of interest to note.

In no. 30 the subject is atmosphere, which is neutral with respect to our comparisons; similarly in no. 32 statement; in such cases we do not have an explicit comparison. But mostly such words as subject nouns will have a modifier which carries the comparison – like extremist label in no. 5, streak of bravery in 13, winning effort in 18, easy-going demeanour in 34, and perhaps amount of work in 19. In other cases both the noun and modifier are required to make the item for comparison, as international collaboration in no. 4, stagnant growth in 10, lifelong fan in 12, collector's passion in 20, professional solicitousness in 26, and linear intensity in 33.

In two pairs of instances the same word appears on both sides – recession in nos. 10 and 11, and paranoia/paranoid in nos. 31 and 33. This shows that the distinction between relative and absolute is not very clear. In 31, for example, paranoia is treated as being within the limits of normal behaviour – but note that its force is lessened by the phrase the atmosphere of paranoia. Pathological is more extreme and unlikely to appear on the left-hand side.

Of the instance with incomplete subjects, the missing word in no. 16 is contention, which is neutral, and the item to be compared is the that-clause that follows. In no. 17 the word is behaviour, also neutral; the embarrassment is indicated in the previous text which shows that the behaviour is that of some unpleasant youth groups. In no. 24 the word is approach, neutral again, and in no. 27 it is idea, followed by a that-clause. In the last instance, no. 35, the subject is this, which refers back to an antecedent which is not fully expressed; the comparative item is in fact a verb, traced back.

In general we conclude that the main reason for the subject nouns to be some distance away is that they themselves are neutral, and the comparison is carried by a longer phrase or clause.

To conclude, our findings are that the subject groups are more varied in structure than the objects, and are regular in their grammatical structure. Whereas it is easy to see the relationship between, for example, love and obsessional (no. 29) or careless and incompetence (no. 7), it seems that in most cases the relationship is either made or focused on or emphasised by the structure. In effect the structure contributes substantially to the making of lexical meaning. (See also Section 12.)

Task 10

Meaning and cotext

A word may have several meanings, and dictionaries present the meanings without giving much guidance as to how they may be differentiated from each other. In Task 1 we looked at <u>block</u> from this point of view, where the meanings are fairly closely related, and in Task 15 we find <u>manage</u>, where the meanings are very closely related. Here we will look at an example of a word whose meanings are quite different – the word <u>lap</u>.

A good modern dictionary will probably suggest that there are three quite separate words that have the form <u>lap</u>. One is a part of the human body, a posture that is made when you sit on a chair; the second is to go once round a track or circuit, as in many sports; and the third is to do with the sound that a moving liquid makes when it touches something solid, or vice versa. There are sub-meanings of at least the second and third of these, but we will start with the general picture.

Let us examine a short concordance for <u>lap</u> with these meanings in mind, **10_lap.doc**.

1. Do you find instances of all three meanings in the concordance? In roughly equal numbers?

2. Identify the instances of the posture meaning, and examine the left cotext, particularly the word immediately to the left. Is there evidence of a special selection here?

3. Follow this up with a look at the words which precede those that you have just examined, and ask the same question – is there regularity of choice here again?

4. Now look at the immediate right cotext of <u>lap</u>; before you get to the words, comment on the punctuation of the "posture" phrases, and associate your observations with the other findings so far.

5. The remaining instances we assume are of the "circuit" meaning. Check this, looking for perhaps small variations.

6. Examine the cotexts of the remaining instances and record any choices of word or phrase that seem to be associated with the "circuit" meaning of <u>lap</u>.

7. Let us look more closely at the collocation <u>last lap</u>. Consult the datafile **10_lastlap.doc** and report on the choices that surround the collocation and their effect on the meaning.

8. Summarise the role of corpus evidence in making distinctions in meaning.

Datafile 10_lap.doc

#		lap	
1	(Albereto spun). Lap ten: sixth. Lap eleven: sixth. Lap		twelve: fifth
2	are pig-awful things to drive. And lap after lap after	lap	off the track by
3	a bunch of bananas. But no one ran a	lap	short. Athletics: Organisers in lap
4	within ten seconds, and after another	lap	he and Phil were below nine minutes a
5	very well. I set fastest lap and by	lap	88 had taken second place and was clo
6	just long enough for me to set fastest	lap	, at 74.5 mph. John took over for a
7	moved up several places in the final	lap	and achieved personal bests, Mayock
8	he afternoon, with her weaving in her	lap	and the toddlers in her care laughing
9	with a bowl of bread and milk on her	lap	, Magnus at her feet on the rag rug,
10	him. He finally laid his head on her	lap	and let the sounds of grief flow. Af
11	the wash of shadows collected in her	lap	. 'Was it you set fire to your house
12	last lap and er Oh. I limped the last	lap	. Oh. Oh dear.
13	lucky to get a clear road on my last	lap	– because it was my second run on my
14	rs off like an infantryman on the last	lap	of the retreat from Moscow. But he i
15	ing that everything would fall into my	lap	, as if by accident. She was now hap
16	ed to a halt at the end of the opening	lap	after a dramatic accident when Ukyo K
17	ttle boy went to sit in his father's	lap	. His publishers called him this morn
18	wo knitting needles from Miss Clare's	lap	, he set them crosswise on the carpet
19	tured to the plate in her daughter's	lap	. "I'm sure I can hear your stomac
20	six-year-old who can fit into a man's	lap	, and a thirteen-year-old who fits pe
21	en patiently sitting in his mother's	lap	, to start wriggling, and she lunged
22	her hands folded in her twilled silk	lap	, her face set and stony under a brim
23	a problem but then halfway round the	lap	I lost the electronic throttle, whic
24	hands were twisting and turning in the	lap	of her skirt. As if conscious of the
25	off all the prize money. We were to	lap	the speedbowl anti-clockwise, left
26	your bunk. Put your notebook on your	lap	. Where's your notebook?"
27	twisting round and grunting in your	lap	. For creatures that weighed no more

Datafile 10_lastlap.doc

#	left context	keyword	right context
1	fortifying themselves for the	last lap	. Helen sat at a back table. She was
2	nurse Rob's car along. Into the	last lap	I thought I was safe with a six-second
3	final into the last corner of the	last lap	I had another piston fail which let
4	any marked attention. Then on the	last lap	into Nanking she fell thoughtful, and I
5	leap to Odysseus' eye when, on the	last lap	of his voyage, the helmsman, spying
6	never missed a beat and on the	last lap	along the hump-back straight in a
7	his unsuspecting team mate on the	last lap	. Pironi always maintained – despite
8	him on the back straight on the	last lap	, going into Stowe corner. I went to the
9	told me that: he was crying on the	last lap	. He went a bit wild afterwards.'
10	dramatically, especially on the	last lap	: 'There was no reason to carry on going
11	I arrived in Leopoldville on the	last lap	of a tour of mainly Francophone West
12	when he suffered a puncture on the	last lap	. Graham Walker, who was to finish
13	up their willing horses and race the	last lap	of the journey in order to get their
14	of a joke till I made them run the	last lap	of over 300 yards. They were all so
15	The engine was working well. The	last lap	with the second set of tyres was really

Task 10

Key

1. There are plenty of meanings one (posture) and two (circuit) but none of the third (liquid). This is not an oddity of the sample, because I have taken many samples from several corpora and I have only very rarely come across the third meaning. So we recognise that there are substantial differences in the frequency of meanings – the first and second seem to be more than ten times as frequent as the third. And since the third meaning divides into the liquid making the sound, water lapping on the side of a boat or the shore, and an animal like a cat or dog drinking, instances of each sub-meaning will be rare indeed.

2.

No.	Cotext
8	her
9	her
10	her
11	her
15	my
17	his father's
18	Miss Clare's
19	her daughter's
20	a man's
21	his mother's
22	her twilled silk
24	the lap of her skirt
26	your
27	your

The regularity of selection of a possessive is remarkable – a COLLIGATION that is clearly part of the creation of this meaning. There are seven possessive adjectives just in front of <u>lap</u>, featuring <u>her</u>, and five modifying noun groups ending with <u>'s</u>. One instance – no. 24 – is of a nominal structure that is closely associated with the others, the definite article in front of the noun and an <u>of</u>-phrase following it. Number 22 is unusual because there are two other modifiers between the possessive and the noun, but it can readily be seen as a variation.

Note that in the <u>'s</u> type the possessive adjective tends to be realised, emphasising the personal side of this meaning – two have <u>his</u> and one has <u>her</u>; also no. 22 has <u>her</u> as well. So of the fourteen instances of this meaning, a possessive adjective is found in twelve, including four where there is already a possessive.

3. The word in front of the possessive is in each case a preposition – in eight times, on three times, into twice and from once. So on the basis of this evidence the word lap occurs in English only as the object of a preposition, and not as subject or object. If you try to make up a sentence with lap as subject ("Darling, what a beautiful lap you have" or "My lap is sore") it is intelligible but sounds extremely odd. I have found one instance in a corpus of lap as object – she patted her lap invitingly – which suggests there may be more, and US speakers say they are not surprised by this kind of usage.

4. In eleven instances there is a punctuation mark just after lap, indicating the end of a construction; six are commas and five are full stops. Two of the instances that do not have this feature have the word and immediately following lap, and these on examination turn out to be similar boundaries to the comma. Among the other instances, only three are followed by punctuation marks, so we can conclude that to end a major structural unit is a very prominent and distinctive part of the way this meaning of lap is deployed.

This observation correlates with the finding that the use of lap seems to be confined to a position in a prepositional phrase, which is often the final element of a structure, in the place where adverbials tend to occur. So instead of saying merely that one of the three main meanings of lap is to do with a posture of the human body, we can now say that we have identified a three-part phrase which makes that meaning and is usually an adverbial element in the clause. The phrase has the lexicogrammatical structure of:

PREPOSITION POSSESSIVE-ADJECTIVE NOUN = lap

5. There is one clear case of a lap that is not a circuit – no. 14. Here it means the last stage of a journey.

6.

No.	Cotext	Category of meaning
1	ten, sixth, eleven, twelve, etc.	numbers
2	lap after lap	circuit
3	Athletics	sport
4	fastest, 88	speed, numbers
6	fastest, 74.5, mph	speed, numbers, measures
7	places, final, bests	competition, measures
12	last	measures
13	last, second	measures
16	opening, accident	public display
23	halfway round, throttle	measures, motor
25	prize money, anti-clockwise	competition, circuit

Conclusion

From a semantic point of view there is plenty of evidence here of the main aspects of the "circuit" meaning of lap, in the numbering and measuring, and the background of competition and speed. There is not sufficient regularity in this small sample for us to work out reliable statements of cotext, and there is a clear overlap of cotext in no. 13, on my last lap. The presence of last lap is a very reliable indicator that we are not talking about posture, but the occurrence of an adjective in this position, while uncommon, also occurs in the "posture" meaning, as shown in no. 22. Also in no. 13 the preposition on is particularly associated with the "posture" meaning, and there is a possessive adjective where the first meaning would expect to find one.

7. All the instances here take the definite article, which is by far the most likely determiner in general for this phrase. There are four clear instances of the "last stage of a journey" meaning (nos. 1, 4, 5 and 11). In no. 1 we are in a bar, and the event is some social ordeal, not a journey at all; in no. 4 the phrase into Nanking indicates a journey, and in no. 5 of his voyage, as well as Odysseus and the helmsman. In no. 11 everything following lap describes an African journey. In contrast seven instances have the "circuit" meaning (nos. 2, 3, 6, 7, 8, 12 and 15). Mostly they are to do with motor racing, and the vocabulary of car, piston, straight, corner (especially a named corner like Stowe), puncture, engine and tyres is indicative.

Given the brevity of the short quotation in these instances, nos. 9 and 10 could instantiate either meaning, but the wider cotext in each names a motor racing driver; no. 13 includes the word race, which suggests "circuit", and journey, which suggests "stage", so it is not surprising that the occasion for this instance is unusual; here is the wider cotext:

> In the west of Ireland there is a tradition that the last corpse into the graveyard must sweep and keep it tidy. If it should happen that two funerals occur at the same time, the cart-drivers whip up their willing horses and race the last lap of the journey in order to get their man in first.

Number 14 also describes a situation analogous to circuit training, where there is no competitive element nor a sense of a goal being reached, so its similarity to the other "circuit" instances is not great.

We might give up at this point and say that there are minor differences of emphasis, that the "circuit" meaning is just a special case of the more general "stage" one, and there is no way of distinguishing them beyond that. However, there are indications of formal differences noted above, sufficient to justify a more detailed enquiry.

There is a difference in SEMANTIC PROSODY between the two, and that is why it is worth pursuing the distinction. The "circuit" meaning is part of a fairly objective vocabulary of measurement, and it can be used just to indicate the position in a race when something happened; here the last lap is no different from the sixth lap or the twenty-fifth. But in the "stage of a journey" meaning the lap is not clearly defined or measured, and there is a definite extra feeling of coming towards the end of a struggle, having overcome tough obstacles, a sense of growing achievement.

Of course, such a meaning of achievement, etc., can also be relevant to the last lap of a race, so the distinction is ultimately not between "circuit" and "stage" but between measurement and conclusion of a strenuous event. The distinction in form is not clear with so few instances, but there are at least indications.

Our investigation is typical of the state of corpus study at the present time – a large and fairly obvious distinction such as that between the "posture" and "circuit" meanings including lap shows that the cotexts are typically distinctive, enough in most cases to determine the meaning. Then a subtler distinction in last lap appears, and a probe into that yields signs of a further distinction in meaning that we can appreciate but not state formally as yet. Within each of those sub-meanings there is a likelihood of an even subtler distinction; in the "circuit" meaning there is no. 14, and in the "stage" meaning there is no. 1. We lack the evidence to pursue this any further, but there is no reason why this finding of ever-subtler distinction should not continue until we end up with the obvious conclusion that each instance has its own uniqueness of meaning. On that journey we will have described a great deal of the way in which language makes meaning.

8. A corpus search is sensitive to frequency, and so in the first instance it will highlight the most common types of pattern that it detects. In this small exercise, only two of the three meanings usually associated with lap have appeared. The absence of the third meaning may be a consequence of nothing more serious than the inherently greater frequencies of nouns over verbs; a search confined to verbal instances of lap shows that the third meaning is quite prominent.

The "posture" meaning is created by a phrase which consists minimally of a preposition, usually on, a possessive, usually an adjective, and the word lap, in that order. The "circuit" meaning is identified by the occurrence of words and phrases of measurement and numbers, along with the characteristic vocabulary of competitive sport, particularly motor sport. The phrase last lap shows more delicate distinctions in meaning that we can only point to in this study.

Also missing from our small sample are instances of a few familiar phrases that include the word lap. Many English speakers, asked for a sentence with the word lap in it, will use the phrase in the lap of luxury or in the lap of the gods. Again, it is no more than the arithmetic of the corpus that means that a phrase of several words is less likely to appear than a single word or a phrase that allows a lot of variation.

So, depending on its size and constitution, the corpus contains evidence of patterns of cotext that either form part of a compound lexical item such as PREP + POSSESSIVE + lap, or support one of the other meanings; ever more subtle meanings peep through as the search becomes more focused, and idiomatic phrases come to the surface despite their fairly low frequency.

LEVEL 3

Task 11

Words difficult to define

This task explores a relationship between words and their meanings. From a dictionary we get the idea that a word has one or more meanings, and when that word is selected in a text, it delivers its meaning. If it has more than one meaning, then the lexicographer has to decide how to distinguish them, and this problem is illustrated in Sections 1, 10, 15 and 17. Here the word we have chosen has only one meaning, so there is no problem in that area; we are free to explore how the meaning is associated with the word and how it is delivered when the word is used.

The word for this task is budge, a verb of middling frequency, familiar to all fluent users of English. Most dictionaries have a problem in defining its meaning, and it is useful at this point to consult one or two dictionaries of English to see what they say. Here is a typical definition from a well-known dictionary (*Longman Dictionary of Contemporary English*):

to (cause to) move a little

The phrase in brackets is a kind of convention in dictionary language which we can expand into:

to move a little
OR
to cause to move a little

– that is to say, we can either talk about something moving itself, or of something else moving it; notice that the movement is small.

We will return to this definition after we have studied a concordance to budge, which is to be found in the datafile **11_budge.doc**. The concordance is alphabetically ordered at two "words" to the left of the word budge; notice that the computer has problems with what is a word, and it regards the shortened negative verbs like can't as two words, leaving n't as an English word, and curious forms like ca and wo. The procedure of deciding on what counts as a word is called TOKENISATION; whatever decision is taken produces results that do not entirely match our intuitions, because people do not like to think that "word" is rather an abstract concept. This difference between the human way of seeing language and the machine one has to be remembered throughout corpus study, because it can affect our interpretations of the results of queries.

1. Given the computer's idea of a word, find the commonest word form immediately to the left of budge, and check that it is more frequent than any

immediately to the right. Then list the other repeated word forms; can you put them into groups on the basis of some feature they share? What is the biggest group?

2. Pick the biggest group and consider whether there are any shared features with other lines in the concordance. How does the normal environment of budge affect its meaning?

3. Now look at position N–2; apart from the nine lines with refuse or refused there, what kind of word occurs, and how often? Can you relate the "refuse" lines to the others?

4. Consider the modality choices in a little more detail. What different kinds of modality are there? How do they relate to the meaning of budge?

5. In which lines is the verb budge transitive? Build this feature into your description.

6. In how many lines does the word budge end a sentence or clause? When the clause with budge continues, what kind of structure occurs? How do you relate this to the meaning of budge? We have already dealt with the transitive clauses, so in those lines look beyond the object for a continuation.

7. The problem involving the word budge can be either a physical event or a social position, usually a point of view. So far we have not required to make this distinction, which is between LITERAL and the FIGURATIVE meaning. The last analytical job is to build in this distinction, watching to see if it correlates with any of the other classifications that we have made. Try to fit it into your description.

8. Finally, go back to the problem of the lexicographer. Is it really sensible to explain the meaning of budge on its own when it interacts so much with other choices in its environment? Can you pick out a phrase or a set of phrase types that can be defined, and that together account for the way budge operates?

Datafile 11_budge.doc

1	now. We wo n't none of us be able to budge tomorrow.' They sat at their tea
2	.90 caliber pezzonovante. You ca n't budge him, not even with money. He has
3	and hesitated. He knew he could n't budge Ben Canaan. He walked to the alcove
4	be so heavy that two horses could not budge it even in moist earth. Although
5	to do so, but she knew she could not budge me from my view. We spent several
6	out of the packet. When it did not budge he shook it more fiercely like 'a
7	It was a dismissal. Bonasera did not budge . Finally, sighing, a good-hearted
8	at the doorknobs the doors did n't budge or even rattle. 'Oh, my God!'
9	wooden door of the museum. It did n't budge . Hastily, I looked round for a
10	neither death nor? disease could budge her. She wrote a cheque for more
11	off scrubbers' hands before it would budge . It was rumoured to be make-work to
12	sat in a corner; I determined not to budge from it until closing-time. I also
13	between the duellists and refuse to budge . Often to everyone 's great relief
14	might be out of his mind and refuse to budge . In that case, the Vice-President
15	he recognizes it, he 'll refuse to budge off that stool where he 's sitting
16	another snail near him he refused to budge , even in the mating season. I often
17	the wings of the eagle and refused to budge . after three thousand years of wait
18	blow. The virus fanciers refused to budge . Whatever the diagnosis, my recovery
19	up to a point but he refuses to budge on design principles he knows to be
20	The humanity here just refuses to budge ." "That 's ridiculous," says
21	me into the dining room, refusing to budge , so that no one else budged, and
22	the coroner himself are gawn 't' budge on that. In the firrst place,
23	it with my shoulder, but it will not budge . I go to the backdoor. I find that
24	side, but still the snake will not budge . He keeps banging it on the head
25	afternoons when the thermometer wo n't budge above minus twenty." "And those
26	pressure any delegation. They wo n't budge from that position." "What a
27	at they might, the British would not budge from their immigration policy. In
28	away louder than ever. I would n't budge either, or come back, till a boy
29	tried the idea on him. He would n't budge . He seemed to have already faded
30	the following months and would not budge – "What 's done can not be undone
31	emergencies. But Mr Volcker has yet to budge on changing his controls over domestic

Task 11

Key

1. The commonest word form at position N−1 is <u>to</u>, with twelve instances. This is much commoner than <u>on</u> (3) on the right at N+1. The other repeated word forms at N−1 are <u>n't</u> (8) and <u>not</u> (8); we take these to be very similar – really variant forms of the same word. We can therefore combine them into a group of simple negatives, which at a total of sixteen is larger than the occurrence of <u>to</u>. (See the Glossary under SPAN for an explanation of the position notation.)

2. We are looking for indications of negatives in other lines. Numbers 1, 10 and 12 contain negatives (<u>won't</u>, <u>none</u> in no. 1, <u>neither</u>, <u>nor</u> in 10 and <u>not</u> in 12), still on the left-hand side but at N−3 or even farther away from <u>budge</u>. They can be added in to the group. So too can the lines which have the verb "refuse" at N−2; in fact "refuse to budge" is the commonest phrasal pattern in the concordance.

It is quite clear that the meaning of "refuse" has a negative quality; the difference in meaning between no. 29 <u>He wouldn't budge.</u> and no. 16 <u>. . . he refused to budge . . .</u> is very slight. Number 29 uses a grammatical form of negation and no. 16 uses a lexical form; the effect is almost identical. (See the Glossary under LEXICALISED.) So instead of remaining strictly within the grammar and saying that the nine lines with "refuse to budge" are positive, and most of the others negative, we say that 28 of the 31 lines are negative.

Cases for comment

The remaining lines will be examined one by one. Number 11 is too short for a clear decision; it concerns the difficulties in removing stains from the skin, and indicates that the stains resisted efforts to remove them for some time. This is neither grammatical nor lexical negation, but the meaning of the line is compatible with the negative quality of the others. It is quite different from, for example, "So we just budged the stains with a little soap and water." – which is a ridiculous sentence in English.

Number 22 is a simulation in writing of a regional dialect of English. It fits in reasonably well with the description as a whole, but needs special statements on every point – for example "t" is the equivalent of "to" in normal written English. There is no negative expressed within the line, but it is fairly clear that there is a negative – probably <u>neither/nor</u> – on the left-hand side. Because of its non-standard nature it will be ignored for the rest of this study.

Number 31 is negative in meaning – Mr Volcker has not yet budged. It is a grammatical negation but without an obvious negative word choice. The meaning arises from the structure <u>has to</u> and the adverb <u>yet</u>.

Conclusion

This consideration of the words coming just before <u>budge</u> establishes quite clearly that it occurs in the environment of a negative; the two main ways of expressing the negative are (a) by the normal use of a negative word like <u>not</u>, and (b) by the selection of the verb <u>refuse</u>, followed by <u>to budge</u>. The very small number of lines that do not precisely match this prescription nevertheless have something negative expressed just before <u>budge</u>.

We can now see why there is a difficulty in defining <u>budge</u> in a dictionary – the unit to be defined is "negative + <u>budge</u>". It is not "moving" that should be the focus of the definition but "*not* moving".

3. Modal verbs are frequent – <u>ca(n't)</u>, <u>could</u> (3), <u>will</u> (2), <u>wo(n't)</u> (2) and <u>would</u> (4). To these we should add two that we have already met in nos. 10 (<u>could</u>) and 11 (<u>would</u>), making a total of 14. In no. 1, <u>able to</u> is very similar to the modal "can". In no. 12, the verb <u>determined</u> is a lexicalisation of the same meaning as <u>would</u>, and this recalls the lines with "refuse", because refusing is not only negative but also has the "would" meaning.

We have now identified 25 of the 30 lines as having modality in some form. Of the remainder, the auxiliary <u>did</u>, which is necessary when there is no modal with a verb and it is negative, occurs four times, and no. 31 also has no indication of modality. So on these figures modality is chosen with <u>budge</u> in over 80% of the cases.

4. There are two main kinds of modality in these instances – what we may call "ability" and "determination". The lines divide as follows:

ability: <u>able</u>, <u>can't</u>, <u>could</u> – 6
determination: <u>will</u>, <u>won't</u>, <u>would</u>, <u>determination</u>, <u>refuse</u>, <u>refused</u> – 19
(neutral): <u>did</u>, etc. – 5

Anything or anyone that cannot be budged is not moving because it is unable to; anyone or anything that will not budge is not moving because it is engaged in preventing the movement. When we are talking about being physically stuck, the use of <u>will</u>, <u>would</u> is fanciful, as in no. 25, where free will is ascribed to a thermometer. The normal use of this type of modality is to refer to the stubbornness of people in discussion and decision, as in no. 27, and in this meaning it overlaps with "refuse to". In the case of animals, as in no. 24 concerning a snake, it will always be unclear whether the animal genuinely refuses or is unable to move.

5. Here is a table of the lines where the transitivity of <u>budge</u> is given, along with the modality:

Line	Transitivity	Modality
1	intrans	able
2	trans	can't
3	trans	could
4	trans	could
5	trans	could
6	intrans	did
7	intrans	did
8	intrans	did
9	intrans	did
10	trans	could
11	intrans	would
12	intrans	determined
13	intrans	refuse
14	intrans	refuse
15	intrans	refuse
16	intrans	refuse
17	intrans	refuse
18	intrans	refuse
19	intrans	refuse
20	intrans	refuse
21	intrans	refuse
23	intrans	will
24	intrans	will
25	intrans	won't
26	intrans	won't
27	intrans	would
28	intrans	would
29	intrans	would
30	intrans	would
31	intrans	has yet to

From this table we can see that transitivity goes with the "ability" modality; no. 1 seems to go against this, but it is an odd line, and it has the modal <u>won't</u> in it as well as the phrase <u>able to</u>. This distinction relates to the bracketed phrase in the definition quoted in the introductory paragraph: "(cause to)". It shows why the exclamation "I can't budge!" would sound so unusual in English.

6. In thirteen lines there is a continuation of the clause with <u>budge</u>. The commonest type is a prepositional phrase where <u>from</u> (4) is the main preposition, with <u>on</u> (2), <u>above</u> and <u>off</u>. This phrase refers to the LOCATION of the incident, whether physical or social.

So we must make a note in the description that a location can, optionally, be specified, both in transitive and intransitive clauses and in those expressing ability or determination. There are no instances here of a choice of location with a clause of neutral modality, but this is probably a result of the small number of lines of this type (4).

Of the remaining continuations, two begin with the adverb <u>even</u> and the preposition <u>in</u>, and refer to a local condition relevant to the incident which one might have expected to alleviate the situation – like <u>moist earth</u>, which might make moving a heavy object somewhat easier, or <u>the mating season</u> for snails, which should tempt them to get on the move. This is a very small indication of what could be another optional element, to intensify the meaning of the central verb complex.

The other three continuations are not apparently related to the choice of <u>budge</u> as the verb. <u>Either</u> and <u>or</u> are rhetorical choices in the sentence structure with full freedom of operation, and <u>tomorrow</u> is a time adjunct, which can be expected in any narrative clause. In fact, the scarceness of time adjuncts is perhaps more significant than the one that occurs, because it points to the fact that we are more likely to time the successful movement of an object or a person than the continuation of their being stuck.

We should note that <u>yet</u> in no. 31 is also a time adjunct, and that in no. 17 the full stop could be a misreading of a comma by an electronic scanner, so that the occurrence of time adjuncts is not perhaps as rare as we thought.

7. The first point to note is that there are a number of doubtful cases. It is interesting that the phraseology round about <u>budge</u> does not clearly indicate the nature of the problem in eight cases. My analysis is rather tentative, and I have made three columns, one being indeterminate; despite that I have classified several lines as physical or social without being entirely confident. These have a query in front of them.

Physical	Social	Not sure
1	2	3
4	5	7
6	10	14*
8	13?	
9	18?	
11	19	
12	26	
15	27	
16	28	
17?	29	
20?	30	
21	31	
23		
24		
25		

Case for comment

In the above table no. 14 is asterisked because it really concerns both the physical and the social simultaneously. It concerns what happens if the President of the United States goes mad and refuses to give up his power and position. If he continues to occupy physically the space that he normally does as President that is one interpretation – he would have to be forcefully ejected. If he continues to act socially as President that is the other interpretation, and announcements would have to be made to explain his loss of authority. It is difficult to separate these two interpretations because both are precisely relevant, and the problem for the people who have to deal with this situation embraces both aspects.

There is a noticeable correlation between the social meaning of budge and the modal category of determination, especially where the modality is realised by would.

8. The characteristic use of budge is with a negative and a modal. There are two aspects of the modality – ability and determination, and the majority of instances make this choice. With an ability modal the structure is likely to be transitive (on the evidence we have, which is not conclusive). Optionally a position can be expressed, either physical or social; if social it usually concerns stubbornness in discussion.

The outline of my dictionary entry for budge would be as follows. (This is a general frame – naturally it would be adapted to the size and intended user of each particular publication.)

budge, verb.

This word is always used with a negative of some sort, whether grammatical or lexical. Normally there is also a modal of:

(a) ability:
If you **cannot budge** something, it is stuck.
two horses could not budge it even in moist earth.

(b) determination:
If something or someone **wouldn't budge** or **refused to budge**, they rejected all attempts to move them.
he'll refuse to budge off that stool. . . . They won't budge from that position.

Notes: the ability choice goes with a choice of transitive; the expression of position (*off that stool, from that position*) is an option; the phrases can be used to express either a physical problem or a social one.

Task 12

Ad hoc meaning

Most sentences contain a unique combination of words; only a few conventional remarks for commonly occurring social occasions are likely to recur in exactly the same form. Grammars and dictionaries describe how meaning arises largely by erecting a framework of choice which shows the word acquiring elements of meaning as the choices become more specific. So the word "the" in English is one of several DETERMINERS; among the determiners are the ARTICLES, of which there are two, and "the" is the DEFINITE ARTICLE. So its route to meaning is:

DETERMINER → ARTICLE → DEFINITE

Similarly a "table" is first classified as a movable object in a room, then as one of the large movable objects called items of furniture, and finally as one with a flat top for putting things on or sitting at.

When several words come together in a linear sequence, they interact with each other, and new meanings are produced which are not in the dictionaries, because they only arise in the unique combination of choices in a single sentence.

This task is the examination of the various choices that occur around the word *veritable*, and how they make their meanings. We begin with the most regular and obvious patterns and gradually look deeper into the patterning of this word.

1. Study the file **12_veritable1.doc**. These are all the examples of the word <u>veritable</u> in a corpus of twenty million words. Note the prominent pattern immediately to the left of the node. What is it?

2. There are several exceptions. Try to explain the reasons for each one, but do not be surprised if they do not all have an easy explanation.

3. Now look to the right of the node word, and make a list of the nouns that <u>veritable</u> modifies, and any other modifiers, or qualifying phrases that occur just after the noun. Find the dominant patterns. Add to this the syntactic role of the noun phrase that includes <u>veritable</u>. How often is it the subject or object of a verb? The complement of a verb like "be", "appear", etc.? In a prepositional phrase?

4. Consider the meaning of the whole phrase:

<u>a</u> + <u>veritable</u> + NOUN

Is there a consistent element of meaning that you note in all, or almost all, the instances? Does this help to explain the remarkably frequent occurrence of the indefinite article a? You may find that looking at the file **12_veritable_colls.doc** will help; here is a list of the nouns that collocate significantly with veritable.

5. Given the presence of this particular kind of meaning, we will now use it to classify the noun headwords. Keep **12_veritable_colls.doc** in front of you for guidance, and pick out any nouns that seem to correlate well with this meaning. Then turn to **12_veritable2.doc** and repeat the search; because so few nouns are repeated we are searching 64 rather than 29 instances.

6. What is the role of the proper names?

7. Which nouns have a fairly common figurative or metaphorical use that is selected here? In **12_veritable_colls.doc** there seem to be a large number of such nouns – army, flood, explosion, mountain, forest and arsenal from the first column only.

8. Which nouns do not normally have a figurative meaning but in combination with veritable acquire one? In **12_veritable_colls.doc** the words industry, revolution, museum, library and machine are of this kind.

9. Of those that are left, some show veritable used just as an emphasiser – note these, and consider the rest individually. How do they relate to the framework a veritable . . . , which anticipates that they will be emotionally charged nouns which are new in the context? At this point also list those words where your decisions do not coincide with the Key.

10. When nouns are transposed metaphorically, they often occur followed by an "of"-phrase that indicates their new provenance. This is not so likely if the metaphorical use is reasonably well established in the language. Go through the two concordances and note all the instances of the pattern

veritable + NOUN + of + NOUN PHRASE

(for the first concordance this is already available in the Key to §3).

11. We will now relate these instances to the classification of the nouns in §5–9. Let us assign symbols to these categories of noun.

§5: the normal meaning of the noun correlates with the meaning required by veritable. Code F (= Fits)
§7: there is a suitable meaning available and veritable selects it. Code S (= Selects)
§8: there is no suitable meaning available and the presence of veritable requires that one is created. Code C (= Creates)
§9: veritable is used as an emphasiser only. Code E (= Emphasises).

The proper names found in §6 can be redistributed among the other categories – how would you do that?

Note the codes of the instances of "of" phrases and see if there is any tendency for them to be associated with one or more categories of meaning-relationship.

12. To bring this task to a close, study the third concordance, **12_veritable3.doc**, noting how far it confirms the various observations we have made about the other two samples, and classifying the nouns according to the coding established in §10. Make a final statement about the way combinations of <u>veritable</u> and a noun it modifies make meaning in a text that is local and unique.

Datafile 12_veritable1.doc

1   gift – a jewel beyond the dream of Scheherazade." " Veritable ?" Arenskaya asked briskly."
2   pieces had a golden sovereign in its midst! A veritable God-send! We really lived fo
3   on earth, or the ugliest; the worst slut or a veritable Mrs Beeton; a mad and
4   with his liquor, and his toilet descended like a veritable Niagara, immediately beyond
5   was still with us, in this or that rented car. A veritable Proteus of the highway, with
6   to the shadows "Is small," she said. "Must be veritable . " She retired with her
7   will be surprised to see that his hands perform a veritable ballet of airborne movements
8   celebration in town judging by the firecrackers, veritable bombs, that exploded all
9   Village Hall, I'm sure the audience has a veritable host of fascinating question
10 troubadour, Guillaume, Count of Poitou; the " veritable love breviary" Roman de la
11 Lo at the time still had for the cinema a veritable passion (it was to decline
12 , then all we have to look forward to is a veritable 'technocracy of the ruins'.
13 or some rich and precious metal. In this shrine, a veritable Byzantine Fort Knox, the
14 in most families. You may also need to marshal a veritable array of friends and relative
15 man, woman and child, whilst to invalids it is a veritable boon." Artists like W. R. S.
16 dull from young men's point of view, although a veritable brick so far as pulling her
17 terminal acne. She could see the factory now, a veritable city of red brick buildings
18 a devout Catholic, Mr David Willis, the last of a veritable dynasty of English physicians
19 growth has been a brief, abrupt phenomenon, a veritable explosion. Professional
20 and was drenched in the wind-borne spray of the veritable fountain. The fountain was
21 of the older kibbutzim, had been turned into a veritable garden. As senior member and
22 dressed mainly in a valuable scroll would appear a veritable gift from Allah. I came out of
23 from voting. Pakistan's 1977 elections were a veritable jamboree of fraudulent practic
24 from his house to school, getting to us would be a veritable marathon. Within a week we
25 ejected sperm of a hanged man, and also we had a veritable mermaid, pretty ratty by now,
26 With No Name (Plexus, 84.50 pounds) is a veritable one-man movie industry compare
27 by an iron triangle that forms for their race a veritable prison cell. One side of this
28 capillaries reruptured. Her flesh was a veritable rainbow. She could have
29 after-hour post-mortems. By comparison, Lee was a veritable tape recorder. It soon

Datafile 12_veritable_colls.doc: nouns modified by <u>veritable</u> in order of significance

feast	industry	palace
cornucopia	smorgasbord	machine
treasure trove	banquet	babel
army	revolution	legion
flood	museum	jungle
explosion	aladdin's cave	force
mountain	minefield	nightmare
forest	sea	tower
paradise	library	soul
arsenal		

Datafile 12_veritable2.doc

1	these once verdant heights, it is a	veritable	acropolis. Its southern terrace
2	instantly commends itself as that	veritable	Astolat, the spirt of which all
3	of a venture have created a	veritable	barrage of paperwork and
4	to fire had been given, because a	veritable	barrage opened up. But Brigadier
5	108 contributors were to comprise a	veritable	beauty parade of the great and
6	reports from across the US. Another	veritable	Bible for Yankophiles.
7	stole the show the fealty of a	veritable	clan of family members, and,
8	like, exists. Omnibus are a	veritable	conveyor belt for this sort of
9	an abundance of fleshy warts – a	veritable	crop – scattered across his face
10	the Gulf crisis, which would be 'a	veritable	disaster that could overturn all
11	sex, capitalist society witnessed a	veritable	explosion of sex talk. Underlying
12	a throw rug. We had met up with a	veritable	farewell party of harp seals and
13	garnie and becomes a	veritable	feast: lightly pickled cabbage
14	and . . . you've got the recipe for a	veritable	feast of nourishing pop. Feed on
15	bids were invited for the pair, a	veritable	forest of hands shot into the
16	have turned Lansdowne Road into a	veritable	fortress – the last time they
17	As a result they are driven into a	veritable	frenzy of wholesale helping,
18	PHOTOS – RAYMOND burr was a	veritable	giant of the small screen,"
19	on global warming, there is a	veritable	gulf between what the scientists
20	Mining ban TO A	veritable	gust of sighs of relief,
21	that in a state that could be a	veritable	landslide for the Democrats,
22	long narrow main street becomes a	veritable	motorists' nightmare and those on
23	asphalt shingles. He chronicles a	veritable	museum of fast-food artifacts –
24	and doubts that Othello is a	veritable	Negro. He cannot believe that
25	DON'T HIRE a video as there's a	veritable	non-stop top comedy-movie
26	certainly five kilometres long, a	veritable	paradise for every bicycle rider
27	night Monarch packed to the	veritable	proverbials. People are standing
28	banks which are spearheading a	veritable	revolution in risk management
29	The Grassroots cable programme, a	veritable	revolutionary soapbox, unlike the
30	then, is the result: 'Beaster', a	veritable	rock jihad of a mini-album
31	I'll bet he got your pictures for a	veritable	song She waited. Susan said
32	Alex Haley's Roots saga began, a	veritable	tourist shrine attraction
33	Barnes Foundation could step into a	veritable	treasure house of art, where over
34	into a swashbuckling adventurer, a	veritable	Vendyl Jones. Shapira lost
35	influence of the environment become	veritable	wells of iniquity and crime, to

Datafile 12_veritable3.doc

1	belonged to a separate room, a	veritable	stronghold. The fire and bomb
2	Its windowless walls make it a	veritable	prison; a depressing bunker
3	solemnly perform and exhibit the	Veritable	, Ancient, and Rectified Rite of
4	McCormick and much more, it was a	veritable	music banquet and celebration of
5	points out, there is a	veritable	chasm between what the child
6	houses in the centre may be old,	veritable	antiquities, but still lack
7	was absolute – as powerful as a	veritable	despot; but his power has
8	of newspaper pop writers, a	veritable	spring chicken, but I happen to
9	taken in Silicon Valley. HP is a	veritable	grand-daddy compared with most of
10	crêperies, Le Shop – The	Veritable	Crêperie, 329 Kings Road,
11	even worse is in the pipeline. A	veritable	Ferrari fax is being schemed
12	certainly five kilometres long, a	veritable	paradise for every bicycle
13	Her digestive system is a	veritable	cosmos in nature, the most
14	between 26 and 44 cents a pound, a	veritable	bonanza. In the next decade the
15	Man River, he just keeps rolling, a	veritable	bowling machine of rhythm, loop
16	our new Book Department is a	veritable	cornucopia of delights for all
17	ennui as politicians talked and a	veritable	industry of constitution-making
18	a western sun, the desert air, a	veritable	army of counselors, and a
19	contribution. This book is a	veritable	storehouse of information for the
20	In fact, at the time there was a	veritable	surge of lesbian activity by
21	annually let loose upon the world a	veritable	flood of crap books, all in the
22	the two sides. It all adds up to a	veritable	clash of the Titans, and no
23	approach with care and caution the	veritable	minefield of the ECOs, latter-day
24	bars and a 30 degree embankment, a	veritable	scene out of 4WD heaven, presents
25	Jews, Hindus and Muslims; it is a	veritable	olla podrida of religions, races
26	was Grace Kelly, who became a	veritable	Ice Princess when she gave up
27	Noel stood almost six feet tall – a	veritable	Viking, said one acquaintance. 8
28	a clothes iron. Amid a	veritable	wig shop of wackiness, both
29	of Punk And Disorderly a	veritable	treasure trove of delights aimed
30	Laws, and by all accounts she's a	veritable	livewire. With live drums, bass

Task 12

Key

1. The indefinite article <u>a</u> comes regularly just before the node word.

2.
Cases for comment

- Number 1. This is a passage about two apparently foreign people, and the author is signalling their foreignness by making them speak unusual English. This looks like an instance of the French word "veritable" rather than the English one.
- Number 6. This is another instance of non-native speakers using unacceptable English. The phrase "Is small," is a deliberate breaking of one of the few almost absolute rules of English – that a finite verb should have a subject.
- Number 8. Here the noun is plural, and so cannot have the indefinite article. Such a usage is considered equivalent to the singular noun preceded by <u>a</u>.
- Number 10. Foreign influences again – here almost certainly the French.
- Number 20. Here is a rare occurrence of the definite article, and even stranger because the noun, <u>fountain</u>, is not followed by <u>of</u>. There are very few occurrences of the veritable . . . in any corpus, and in well over 80% of the cases the reason for <u>the</u> is the following <u>of</u>-phrase. The present instance is almost unique.

We will ignore nos. 1, 6 and 10 from now on because they are quite deviant from normal English.

3.

No.	Noun	Modifier(s) and qualifier(s)	Syntactic role of noun group
2	God-send		exclamation
3	Mrs Beeton		one of a series of antitheses
4	Niagara		in a <u>like</u> phrase
5	Proteus	of the highway	probably apposition
7	ballet	of airborne movements	clause object
8	bombs		apposition
9	host	of fascinating questions	clause object
11	passion		clause object
12	technocracy	of the ruins	complement of <u>is</u>
13	Fort Knox	Byzantine	apposition
14	array	of friends and relatives	clause object

No.	Noun	Modifier(s) and qualifier(s)	Syntactic role of noun group
15	boon		complement of is
16	brick		probably complement of "be"
17	city	of red brick buildings	apposition
18	dynasty	of English physicians	in an appositional phrase
19	explosion		apposition
20	fountain		in an of phrase
21	garden		in an into phrase
22	gift	from Allah	complement of appear
23	jamboree	of fraudulent practices	complement of were
24	marathon		complement of be
25	mermaid		clause object
26	movie industry	one-man	complement of is
27	prison cell		complement of forms
28	rainbow		complement of was
29	tape recorder		complement of was

Note that there is a noun following veritable in every instance; this shows it to be an ATTRIBUTIVE adjective. The only repeated pattern within the noun group is that nine of the nouns are followed by an of-phrase. There are no repeated nouns.

The dominant syntactic role is that of complement (10) or object (5) of the clause; the noun group is never subject in this sample. The other frequent syntactic role is that of apposition (6).

4. The effect of this structure is to emphasise the noun greatly, making it sound very dramatic, lexically rich and full of portent. It often involves the extremity of a scale of meaning, the biggest or the best or the most violent. Looking at the file **12_veritable_colls.doc**, we note that feast is a big and special meal, as is banquet and, slightly oddly, smorgasbord, while cornucopia, the horn of plenty, is an unusual and powerful word in English. Other words that seem to be similar in their extravagance of meaning are treasure trove and paradise, Aladdin's cave and nightmare.

The meaning of the indefinite article is to signal that the following noun group is new information, and therefore a potential point of interest. This contrasts with the definite article which signals that the following noun has:

(a) already been introduced into the conversation, or
(b) is obvious in the context, or
(c) is identified by a prepositional phrase or clause that immediately follows it.

Now if the effect of veritable is to make a big fuss about the importance of the noun it modifies, then this meaning correlates well with the "newness" signalled by a. We now appreciate why the combination "the veritable . . ." is very uncommon, and why when it does occur it is nearly always followed by an "of" phrase.

5. In the classification, §5–9, we are in an area of personal taste and judgement, and no two people are likely to make exactly the same decisions; keep notes on where you vary from the personal classification below.

A few of the nouns seem to me to have a strong and almost exaggerated meaning even without the word veritable. These are, in the first concordance, God-send, passion, jamboree and marathon. (The spelling of God-send with capital letter and hyphen is unusual.)

In the second concordance they are disaster, feast (twice), fortress (rather than "castle"), frenzy, giant, paradise and treasure house.

We can say of these choices that they fit very well the expectations set up by veritable. Veritable sets up the expectation of a special kind of noun to follow it, and these are pretty clear cases of that kind of noun.

6. The proper names in the first concordance are:

Mrs Beeton, Niagara, Proteus, Fort Knox

Each refers to a person or place associated with an extreme feature. Mrs Beeton wrote a classic book on housekeeping and cookery that is still in print after a century; the Niagara Falls are exceptionally high; the Greek myth of Proteus tells of his ability to change into the shape of another creature very quickly; and Fort Knox is where the United States keeps its gold reserves, and is known as one of the most heavily guarded places on earth.

In conjunction with veritable these are metaphorical uses, where the notable feature of the person or place is transferred as a quality into the new situation.

In the second concordance the proper names are:

Astolat, Bible, Vendyl Jones

Astolat is a place name from the King Arthur stories; Vendyl Jones is presented here as a swashbuckling adventurer like Indiana Jones; the Bible is felt by Christians to be an authoritative and comprehensive book of moral and spiritual guidance.

7. In the first concordance:

explosion, fountain, rainbow

The use of fountain has already been noted as unusual, and while the word is commonly used metaphorically ("fountain of youth", "fountain of knowledge", etc.) it may not be in this instance.

In the second concordance:

barrage (twice), crop, forest, gulf, landslide, tourist shrine attraction, wells

We can say of these words that they have quite ordinary literal meanings – a landslide is the movement of land down a hill – and also metaphorical meanings where a dramatic element of meaning appears, so that a landslide result in an election is a very big victory for one side. In many of these words nowadays the commonest meaning is the metaphorical one.

In the cotext of the modifier <u>veritable</u>, the more dramatic metaphorical meaning is required. Here we can see <u>veritable</u> determining the meaning of a potentially ambiguous noun, controlling the selection of meaning.

8. In the first concordance:

<u>ballet</u>, <u>bombs</u>, <u>technocracy</u>, <u>brick</u>, <u>city</u>, <u>dynasty</u>, <u>garden</u>, <u>gift from Allah</u>, <u>mermaid</u>, <u>movie industry</u>, <u>prison cell</u>, <u>tape recorder</u>

In the second concordance:

<u>acropolis</u>, <u>parade</u>, <u>clan</u>, <u>conveyor belt</u>, <u>crop</u>, <u>party</u>, <u>museum</u>, <u>revolution</u>, <u>soapbox</u>, <u>jihad</u>

These words have ordinary meanings and are ordinarily used quite unemotionally; when they are placed after <u>veritable</u> this ordinary meaning is not relevant. So the listener or reader has to imagine a metaphorical meaning that will be appropriate for the cotext, and – for this unique instance only – will make sense:

<u>his hands perform a veritable ballet of airborne movements</u>

Something of the grace, beauty, control and energy of the ballet is transferred to the hand gestures of the man talked about in this instance.

The same process of interpretation is used in the other instances. If a factory is called a <u>city</u> then the great size of a city is being highlighted, and that extreme feature is applied to a factory, which is expected to be much smaller. <u>Industry</u> is not usually metaphorical, but it certainly includes the idea of a very large number of people working in the same line of business. As a metaphor it presumably means that an individual was so enterprising and energetic that his efforts seemed to be much more than that of a single person. A <u>tape recorder</u> is not usually metaphorical, but when used of a person it highlights their ability to repeat what has been said – perhaps rather boringly.

9. <u>veritable</u> as emphasiser only:

<u>host</u>, <u>array</u>, <u>boon</u>

There is an older meaning of <u>host</u> – a large crowd of people, angels, etc., from which this modern meaning no doubt derived – but I have classified it here rather than under §7 because the early meaning is no longer current.

Individual instances, second concordance

- Number 20. gust is a brief, weak breeze, and is not the kind of word that we should expect after veritable; "storm" would be more appropriate. But it is a gust of sighs, and sighs are even weaker and shorter than gusts; so it is used ironically here.
- Number 24. Negro has an initial capital letter but is not considered a proper name here; veritable is used in the way that we use "real" or "true" (Tognini Bonelli, 1992). In Shakespeare's play *Othello* the precise racial categorisation of Othello himself, called "The Moor of Venice", is always controversial.
- Number 27. proverbials shows a rather mannered English expression; when someone is aware of using a familiar idiom, they can draw attention to it by replacing an important word by "proverbial". So here the idiom is "packed to the gunwales". Perhaps, since the word "gunwales" is not very common nowadays, the speaker had forgotten it and so substituted the word proverbials for it.
- Number 31. song uses veritable to indicate the presence of an idiom – here "for a song", meaning "a good bargain, very cheap", especially in the phrase "going for a song" – here "got . . . for a . . . song".

Doubtful classifications

- Number 1/19. explosion. This is classed in §7 because it is felt to have distinct literal and metaphorical meanings, but it could also be classed in §5 if all its uses are thought to be "explosive".
- Number 2/28. revolution. This is classed in §8, but could also have been in §5 if you think that the regular meaning of the word has this special charge of drama and emotion.

10. See §11.

11. The proper names can be classified, in my opinion, as follows:

Mrs Beeton	C
Niagara	S
Proteus	S
Fort Knox	S
Astolat	C
Bible	S
Vendyl Jones	C

The "of" phrases are classified as follows:

Proteus of the highway	S
ballet of airborne movements	C
host of fascinating questions	E

technocracy of the ruins	C	
array of friends and relatives	E	
city of red brick buildings	C	
dynasty of English physicians	C	
jamboree of fraudulent practices	F	
barrage of paperwork	S	
beauty parade of the great and . . .	C	
clan of family members	C	
explosion of sex talk	S	
farewell party of harp seals	C	
feast of nourishing pop	F	
forest of hands	S	
frenzy of wholesale helping	F	
giant of the small screen	F	
gust of sighs of relief	(irony)	
museum of fast food	C	
rock jihad of a mini-album	C	
treasure house of art	F	
wells of iniquity and crime	S	

The distribution, given these small numbers, is fairly even, so we can postulate that the "of" phrase is an independent choice from the assignment of meaning-relationship.

12.

No.	Noun	Type	Modifiers and qualifiers	Notes
1	stronghold	S		apposition
2	prison	S		clause object
3	Rite		Ancient and Rectified	of-phrase, ritualistic language
4	banquet	F	music	complement
5	chasm	F		complement
6	antiquities	C	old	complement
7	despot	F		comparison phrase, as . . . as
8	spring chicken	C		apposition
9	grand-daddy	C		complement
10	Crêperie		article the	shop name
11	fax	S	Ferrari	subject; see comments below
12	paradise	F	for every bicycle . . .	apposition
13	cosmos	S		complement
14	bonanza	F		apposition
15	machine	C	bowling, of rhythm	apposition
16	cornucopia	F	of delights	complement
17	industry	C	of constitution-making . . .	
18	army	S	of counselors	apposition
19	storehouse	C	of information	complement
20	surge	S	of lesbian activity	complement

No.	Noun	Type	Modifiers and qualifiers	Notes
21	flood	S	of crap books	clause object
22	clash	F	of the Titans	prepositional object, idiom
23	minefield	S	of the ECOs	clause object
24	scene	C	out of 4WD heaven	apposition; see comments below
25	olla podrida	C	of religions	complement; see comments below
26	Ice Princess	C		complement
27	Viking	S		apposition
28	shop	C	wig, of wackiness	prepositional object; see comments
29	treasure trove	F	of delights	apposition
30	livewire	F		complement

Cases for comment

- Number 11:
  - (a) This phrase is clause subject, which is not common – but there were two instances also in the second concordance.
  - (b) The word whose meaning correlates with veritable is not the noun fax, but the modifier Ferrari. Fax on its own would be coded C. Perhaps the two words should be taken together – there are several instances in this selection where I was unsure whether or not to conflate them.
- Number 24. The word whose meaning correlates with veritable is heaven, which is in a prepositional phrase qualifying the noun.
- Number 25. olla podrida is a Spanish stew which contains a wide range of ingredients.
- Number 28 is one I do not understand, and so I will rely on the conventions we have noted in this task, assuming that it can be interpreted normally. People's appearance or behaviour was so outlandish (wacky) that the writer was reminded of a wig shop where perhaps a bizarre selection of wigs would be on display.

Summary

The new instances match quite well the descriptive framework, and there are no novel cases or widely differing frequencies to note. The categories of "fit" (8), "select" (8) and "create" (10) are all prominent, showing that in a third of the instances new meaning is actually created by the requirement of veritable that its noun group will give a strongly dramatic, exaggerated semantic prosody. Of the nouns that already fit this requirement cornucopia, treasure trove, paradise and banquet are listed in **12_veritable_colls.doc**, and of those that can select such a meaning army, flood and minefield are also included in that file.

Task 13

Grammatical frames

There is a widely accepted distinction in English and other languages between "grammatical" and "vocabulary" words. No-one can say exactly where the line should be drawn, but almost everyone accepts that the words the and apple are of two different kinds. The is a building block of text structure, and while it has a kind of meaning, it is hardly an independent unit of meaning. Apple, on the other hand, has a clear referential meaning, and a dictionary entry for that word is not difficult to write.

Most of the concordances that you will come across – including many of those in this book – are centred on a word or phrase that has lexical content, like apple. Such words make clear and easy starting-points for the exploration of corpus patterning. There have been some studies of so-called "grammatical words", showing that they actually have a clear lexical presence, which amounts to treating them in the same way as "vocabulary" words are treated. This is valuable work, but it is not the whole story; combinations of grammatical words can form repetitive frameworks for phrasal units where the vocabulary words within them vary a great deal. The most frequent combination of words in English within a small SPAN is the ... of ... – the two commonest words in the language. All sorts of vocabulary words fill in where I have put dots, and though there are many that are quite frequent, none is more than a COLLOCATION, rather than part of the CORE. Typical words between the and of are end, middle, heart, rest, number, kind, sort, idea, age and cost.

The core of this expression is in fact the ... of, and the words that come between them are collocates, as are the words that follow them. This is a different kind of unit from those that centre on a single vocabulary word like budge, or a phrase like true feelings.

In this task we will build up an understanding of one of these phraseological units of meaning.

1. Study the datafile **13_asas.doc**, and in particular the word that comes between two occurrences of as. Arrange the instances according to the frequency of this word, ignoring single occurrences at present.

2. Some phrases have a special meaning called IDIOMATIC – see IDIOM. Where a phrase can have an idiomatic as well as a general meaning (like as well as meaning "in addition to" rather than "as healthy as") note how many of each meaning there are. Look at the single occurrences for any instances of less common phrases with idiomatic meanings. Work out the proportion of instances that have an idiomatic meaning.

3. Now look at the instances which do not have an idiomatic meaning. You might expect that to say that something is "as X as" something else is to mean that the two things compared are very similar with respect to X – for example, no. 18. Find all the instances which make this sort of meaning, and comment on the meanings of the rest.

4. Look to the left of the first as and see if there are any repeated patterns of words or word classes. Then summarise what we have discovered about the as . . . as phrase.

5. We are now going to leave aside the idiomatic phrases and explore one of the more complex patterns – the phrase about as . . . as. Look at the datafile **13_aboutasas.doc**; first pick out any cases where you do not think about is part of the phrase. Then consider the meaning of each instance in turn. Use the categories already established to talk about the meaning. Then summarise the trends that you observe.

6. We have now described a situation where a phrase can have either a straight-forward meaning or an ironic one that is the opposite of the straightforward one. The question now to be asked is "how do users of English know which way to interpret the phrase?" First of all, review all the instances you have classified as ironic genuine comparisons. Start with the Z element, and ask yourself whether there are any clues there – for example, if the Z element is absurd as in no. 26, voting an end to [winter], this is clearly a useless activity in itself, and so anything that is said to be as useful as that must be pretty useless.

After this, go back through, ignoring the Z element, and consider whether or not you know before you reach there that the ironic meaning is the most likely. If so, then the meaning cannot arise just in the absurdity of the Z element. Can you suggest a reason for it?

7. We will take one further step in probing into this kind of phrase and its unusual meanings. The datafile **13_aboutasusefulas.doc** contains 21 instances of about as useful as. . . . According to our predictions, most of these should have an ironic meaning. Check this out, and note also, as before, whether the Z element is obviously useless and whether it is necessary to know what it is.

8. Summarise the role of about applied to as . . . as . . . phrases.

Datafile 13_asas.doc

#		as	as	
1	only green in the north; the south was	as	as	arid as ever. Between 1958 and 1963,
2	these two play-offs are about	as	as	big as it gets. I am not stupid," he
3	What about the Cubans? Is – is baseball	as	as	big as I've heard it is with them?
4	policy needed to deal with a problem as complex	as	as	poverty must cover a wide
5	from machinery or fellow workers, is	as	as	erroneous as the idea that the 19th
6	Group pension fund. He said:'	As	As	far as personal guarantees are
7	if that's the case, it is good enough	as	as	far as I'm concerned." Should
8	t need to ask – I'd come too soon,	as	as	far as she was concerned, and I knew
9	s-eye view of corporate Goliaths,	as	as	hilarious as it was incensed. If
10	gasped Colonel Campos The links are	as	as	large as a man's wrist.' Difficult to
11	other input details of this proposal. As	As	long as there is not an absolut
12	There we are. I mean as long as	as	as	you feel that he As long as
13	concentration demanded, she works for	as	as	long as the elements allow. If the
14	usually tolerant of blacks, but only	as	as	long as they are kept inferior," Mr
15	uniquely Japanese (though not nearly	as	as	many as most Japanese and Westerners
16	seems to prejudge the argument, almost	as	as	much as the idea of 'technophobia',
17	the wrong side of the post. It was	as	as	near as Spike came to scoring.
18	some senior advisers were almost	as	as	powerful as ministers, but
19	Previously, we were losing the ball	as	as	soon as it went up field and it was
20	they concede. They must divorce	as	as	soon as possible," was the refrain
21	Loverde-Bagwall and Christopher Sharp,	as	as	well as Maurice Voituriez and of
22	the life within her to think about	as	as	well as her own, Joanne chose the
23	places will suit their tastes and mood	as	as	well as their pockets. 'I am not in
24	of the political community, the weak	as	as	well as the strong. It was for this
25	with British opposition politicians	as	as	well as business leaders.
26	of European imperialistic exploits	as	as	well as one of the most scandalous.
27	settlers. It claims that secular	as	as	well as religious members agree on
28	state (some of which you can touch),	as	as	well as cancerous organs on display.
29	and members of the decorating team,	as	as	well as Ann Grafton and Michael Lock,
30	Dame Barbara Cartland, was there	as	as	well as his mother, Raine Countes

Datafile 13_aboutasas.doc

1   Antonio isn't you're bag and Karachi cinema is   about as   appealing as a repeat of Legends of the
2   He allocates to Hampshire 66,500. That's   about as   close as we come to national government
3   these towering 20-centimetre heels which are   about as   deep as the advert on the right.
4   occasionally when you travel. The two of us   about as   different as is possible to conceive
5   your child's gender, and this watch is   about as   effective as crossing your fingers," says
6   back. Frances would say, How nice, which was   about as   effusive as Frances could get. She tried
7   the Child Support Agency – a valid debate, but   about as   European as a pint of bitter. The law
8   s handsome training headquarters, Kahn looked   about as   frail as Robocop. Presence, he said, was a
9   charming, middle-aged white American attendants   about as   funky as Ena Sharples; The Michael
10 the talks. And the worse news is that this is   about as   good as it ever gets: with so much
11 chances of finding those hubs,' I said, 'are   about as   good as mine are finding a 100S engine
12 good copy, do you? I don't. I thought it was   about as   interesting as reading the back of a
13 lanky 26-year-old in a green paper hat looking   about as   jolly as the joke in his cracker. Even the
14 shark during next year's Games. It found that's   about as   likely as a redback spider turning up on
15 for their benefit. Older Native Americans are   about as   likely as older Anglo Americans to live
16 wine was brought to market, French Kiss lasted   about as   long as Reggie! The party at Standard
17 result of entirely random brain activity and so   about as   meaningful as the messy pattern made when
18 this year is set to account for 8.3% of GDP –   about as   much as in rich Germany. Ludek Rubas, the
19 feeling that you've explored this and disagree   about as   much as you will disagree on this. But
20 instead of each other. They love each other   about as   much as Hitler and Stalin did. In addition
21 staff collect them and drive them here. It's   about as   much as my mum and I can cope with; she
22 The traditional pre-war Sports Car race is   about as   near as you can get in Historic sport to
23 Jesus Christ she said, adding: 'And that's   about as   positive as I can feel about the
24 THIRTY-runner sprint handicaps are   about as   reliable as an election promise when it
25 at his disposal was a piece of kidology   about as   subtle as the former Norway manager's
26 voting to reconstitute the Soviet Union was   about as   useful as voting to declare an end to
27 terms of identifying fresh English talent, is   about as   useful as JR Hartley winning the Booker
28 mightily to listen to what I was talking   about as   well as keep her eye and that other ear on
29 with my G P because you know I can't mess them   about as   well as anything else you know. So
30 attractive on the hustings but quickly becomes   about as   wholesome as cussing in church when

Datafile 13_aboutasusefulas.doc

1. a game plan in boxing is about as useful as a road map in the desert, since
2. history or economics. It's about as useful as a degree in astrology. Well,
3. transport, the car was about as useful as a motorbike, Insp McLeod said.
4. the investigation was about as useful as a train smash. Mr Gibbs,
5. 30–06, the .45 would be about as useful as a rock. Still, it felt good. He
6. without software is about as useful as a machine that exists only as a
7. thinks that Christianity is about as useful as a yeast infection, so I suppose
8. A suede umbrella? Sounds about as useful as a chocolate parasol. In fact,
9. or special privileges. It's about as useful as an MBE. However, let's be
10. faith are probably still about as useful as anything else in surviving a
11. digital broadcasts, will be about as useful as carrying half a house brick
12. fresh English talent, is about as useful as JR Hartley winning the Booker
13. contain seeds that are about as useful as leather is to a starving man.
14. diet with tasty treats is about as useful as locking a sex maniac in a
15. out to rip you off. That's about as useful as me trying to buy a six-bedroom
16. department, is about as useful as posting a surgeon to watch a
17. to save in the 1990s is about as useful as teaching them to drive a horse
18. Nations (an organisation about as useful as teats on a boar) on the 20 cent
19. of the accumulated data is about as useful as the stuff at the bottom of the
20. structures are really only about as useful as the people that run them, and I'
21. the Soviet Union was about as useful as voting to declare an end to

Task 13

Key

1. as well as	10
as long as	4
as far as	3
as soon as	2
as big as	2

2. All instances are of the idiomatic kind except no. 13, where as long as means length of time, and the two instances of as big as, which are understood literally. This means that 18 out of the 30 instances are of idiomatic meanings, which is 60%.

3. Those that conform to expectations are nos. 10, 15, 16, 17 and 18. There is in most of them an extra meaning of "very X"; for example, no. 10 includes the meaning "The links are very large." Number 17 is an exception to this, implying that Spike did not score, or come near to scoring.

The other instances also contain the notion of "very X", but they are not really comparisons. Number 1 means that the south was always very arid, no. 2 that the two play-offs are the biggest, no. 3 that baseball is very popular among Cubans, no. 4 that poverty is a very complex problem, no. 5 that both ideas are quite erroneous, and no. 9 that the view was both very hilarious and very incensed.

4. The only clear pattern is the occurrence of adverbs such as about, nearly and almost, which are expressions of approximation; these are incompatible with as well as and as far as, and occur in four of the seventeen remaining instances – not a very strong pattern until the distinction just made is applied. Of the five instances which seem closest to our "literal" interpretation of as . . . as, three are modified by an adverb; the remaining instance of an adverb is no. 2, about, which on close inspection does not appear to be just indicating approximation.

To summarise so far: most of the as . . . as phrases are idiomatic, and one, as well as, is extremely dominant, accounting for half of the instances. Of the non-idiomatic instances, just over half do not express comparison, but act as intensifiers. Of the remainder, several are modified by nearly or almost, indicating approximation. There is a small loose end in the use of the adverb about in no. 2.

5. In the two instances of as well as, the word about is part of a phrasal verb – talking about in no. 28 and mess them about in no. 29. We will ignore them.

We will now summarise the categories of meaning that we have established, and provide an ad hoc terminology.

Regular: comparing two entities with reference to an attribute and indicating that they are similar with respect to that attribute. As a formula:

Y is about as X as Z

Number 18 is a fairly clear instance of this meaning, which is often found in expressions of measurement.

Regular +: a comparison with the added implication that the attribute is very marked in the entities concerned.

Y and Z are both very X

This type is common with qualitative adjectives, because the choice of adjective often implies that it is a feature of Z at least; so "Y is as big as Z" suggests that Z is known to be big and Y is also big; if Y and Z were not very big then "Y is as small as Z" would be less misleading.

Number 3 is an instance of this meaning – the heels are very deep, and the Z element gives an idea of how deep.

Ironic: a comparison with the added implication that the attribute is not at all characteristic of either of the entities.

Y and Z are both very low in X

As pointed out above, this is rather unexpected – why should someone choose an adjective which is not characteristic of the entities being compared? It produces an ironic meaning – neither X nor Z are at all Y.

Genuine or **False** comparison. There is another feature that cuts across the classification; this is whether the comparison is genuine – that is to say, Y and Z are comparable entities – or false, as in no. 10, as it ever gets, where there is no Z element. Note that in nos. 2 and 22 there are such phrases, but also Z elements.

Idiomatic: for example, as well as. We have already dismissed the two instances of that item, and there are no other phrases with idiomatic meaning in the concordance – it is as if the about made it less likely that there would be idiomatic phrases of this kind.

No.	Adjective	Meaning type	G/F
1	appealing	ironic	G
2	close	ironic	G
3	deep	regular +	G
4	different	regular +	F
5	effective	ironic	G
6	effusive	ironic	F
7	European	ironic	G
8	frail	ironic	G

No.	Adjective	Meaning type	G/F
9	funky	ironic	G
10	good	ironic	F
11	good	ironic	G
12	interesting	ironic	G
13	jolly	ironic	G
14	likely	ironic	G
15	likely	regular	G
16	long	ironic	G
17	meaningful	ironic	G
18	much	regular	G
19	much	regular +	F
20	much	ironic	G
21	much	regular +	F
22	near	regular	G
23	positive	ironic	F
24	reliable	ironic	G
25	subtle	ironic	G
26	useful	ironic	G
27	useful	ironic	G
30	wholesome	ironic	G

Comments

The most remarkable trend in the above table is the number of phrases with ironic meaning – 21 out of 28 instances, 75%. Since the original **13_asas.doc** datafile had none of these, it is likely that by adding <u>about</u> into the phrase, this kind of meaning became more prominent. Only three instances are simply "regular", while four are the augmented variety of regular.

The distribution of Genuine and False comparisons does not correlate well with the other choices, though three out of the four cases of regular+ are False comparisons, and this may be a trend.

Note that in no. 22 the Z element is only hinted at by <u>to</u> at the end of the line. The relevant wider cotext is:

> The traditional pre-war Sports Car race is about as near as you can get in Historic sport to the medieval Knight jousting to protect the honour of his Lady Fayre.

My interpretation of this is that the nearness is adequate to make the comparison (while distant enough to be humorous), so my classification is regular; I agree that an ironic interpretation is possible, if you imagine the Y and Z elements to be ridiculously dissimilar.

6. In the following table the column "Z is nonX" depends a great deal on personal knowledge of the world, and subjective opinion. For example, in no. 1 it is clear that the author considers a repeat of Legends of the Fall as an extremely

unappealing event, but I personally have no knowledge or experience of it – I presume it is a television programme. In such cases I have recorded "not known", and I expect that each person's response in this column will be different.

No.	Adjective	Z element	Z is nonX	Z is not required
1	appealing	a repeat of Legends of the [Fall]	not known	not required
5	effective	crossing your fingers	nonX	not required
7	European	a pint of bitter	nonX	not required
8	frail	Robocop	nonX	required
9	funky	Ena Sharples	not known	not required
11	good	finding a 100S engine	not known	not required
12	interesting	reading the back of . . .	nonX	not required
13	jolly	the joke in his cracker	nonX	not required
14	likely	a redback spider turning up on	not known	not required
16	long	Reggie	not known	required
17	meaningful	the messy pattern made when . . .	nonX	not required
20	much	Hitler and Stalin did	not known	required
24	reliable	an election promise	nonX	not required
25	subtle	the former Norway manager's	not known	not required
26	useful	voting to declare an end to . . .	nonX	not required
27	useful	J R Hartley winning the Booker . . .	nonX	not required
30	wholesome	cussing in church	nonX	not required

Where the status of the Z element is "not required", then it does not matter whether the reader/listener knows it or not. That accounts for most of the instances, leaving just three where this kind of world knowledge is required – nos. 8, 16 and 20 for me. Regarding no. 8 I happen to know that Robocop was an icon of toughness, but with the cotext given the meaning could just as easily be regular. I am able to look at the document as a whole, where it is obvious in the previous 500 words that Kahn is extremely aggressive and formidable, so that resolves the problem. Regarding no. 16, I know neither French Kiss nor Reggie, and the adjective long can occur in several different phrases of the as . . . as type. Again the previous cotext tells me that they are unsuccessful brands of wine; without that knowledge I would not be able to resolve the meaning, but the information is provided in the text. As regards no. 20, I cannot remember any particular love or hate relationship between Hitler and Stalin, but they fought against each other in a major war so in the absence of clear evidence I would guess the meaning is ironic here. The previous cotext in fact makes it clear.

So all the information I need is supplied in the cotext. But this does not explain how, in the cases where I claim that I know before encountering the Z element, whether the meaning is ironic or not. This seems to lie in the combination of about and the adjective chosen. The selection of about, as we have seen, makes it likely that in three cases out of four the meaning will be ironic. Combined with this, the choice of a clearly qualitative adjective such as useful makes the ironic meaning exceptionally probable. Where the adjective is possibly quantitative, like <u>long</u> or <u>much</u>, the previous cotext is needed to clarify the meaning, and also adjectives like <u>frail</u>, which is more of an objective judgement than <u>appealing</u> – that is to say, thousands of people may like the TV programme that is judged unappealing, but few will mistake a frail person for a tough one.

Where the comparison is False, similar conditions of interpretation apply. There is no Z element, but a conventional phrase like <u>as we come</u>, <u>as it ever gets</u>. So we rely entirely on the choice of adjective or the wider cotext.

No.	Adjective	Previous cotext	Evaluation
2	close	He allocates to Hampshire 66,500	inadequate closeness
4	different	happy to be different	pseudo-Z element required
6	effusive	How nice	adjustive + inadequate effusion
10	good	worse news	inadequate goodness
19	much	strong disagreement	clear regular interpretation
23	positive	negative feelings	negative attitude

Note

In no. 4, the conventional phrase <u>as is possible to conceive</u> clearly indicates a regular +.

7.

No.	Meaning type	Z is nonX	Z is not required
1	ironic	nonX	not required
2	ironic	nonX	not required
3	ironic	cotext indicates bike is useless	not required
4	ironic	cotext indicates delicate situation	not required
5	ironic	cotext indicates .45 is useless	not required
6	ironic	nonX	not required
7	ironic	nonX	not required
8	ironic	nonX	not required
9	ironic	could be useful	not required
10	regular	false comparison	not present
11	ironic	nonX	not required
12	ironic	nonX	not required
13	ironic	not known	not required
14	ironic	nonX	not required
15	ironic	nonX	not required
16	ironic	nonX – see note	not required
17	ironic	nonX	not required
18	ironic	nonX	not required
19	ironic	nonX	not required
20	regular	not known	required
21	ironic	nonX	not required

Note

In no. 16 the Z element in full is <u>posting a surgeon to watch a butcher operate on somebody's brain</u>.

Comment

The dominant pattern is that the meaning is ironic; the Z element is obviously useless, but is not required because the combination of <u>about</u> and <u>useless</u> suggests very strongly the ironic meaning. The two instances of regular meaning are thus worthy of inspection. Number 10 has a false comparison, and there is an overall impression that not much is useful in surviving a [tornado], so there is a slight flavour of irony here, but not in the Z element. In no. 20 there is again an overall suggestion that the [bureaucratic] structures are fairly useless, but since it depends on the people that run them, and we are not told how useful they are, this is a fairly neutral comparison. Like a number of instances, the fact that the Z element is not entirely independent of the Y element gives a slant to the meaning – as here, the implication that the limit of usefulness lies in the quality of the people. To follow up this point we would need another investigation.

8. The addition of <u>about</u> to <u>as . . . as . . .</u> phrases makes it very likely indeed that an ironic meaning will be made, and even in those cases where the regular meaning is relevant, there is an over-arching suggestion of "nonX" about the effect of the phrase as a whole. In all probability the results obtained for <u>useful</u> will be repeated with other adjectives of the same kind, qualitative adjectives which do not rely on observables for their validation, but are essentially subjective. There is a strong tendency in the more journalistic writing to think up Z elements which are obviously ridiculous, like a chocolate parasol, but these are not the items which control the interpretation; as the tables show, in most cases the nonX nature of Z is predictable before we encounter it.

Task 14

Hidden meanings

Often the use of a word in a particular cotext carries extra meaning of an emotive or attitudinal nature; if you have a sporting victory, and in the presence of your opponents you call it a "walkover", you insult them, although the victory may have been very easy. This kind of meaning is sometimes called "connotation" (as against "denotation" for the ordinary meaning of the word), and sometimes this kind of meaning is called "pragmatic" meaning.

We will see in this book that this kind of meaning is structurally important, and essential for the understanding of language text. We will call it SEMANTIC PROSODY – semantic because it deals with meaning, and prosody because it typically ranges over combinations of words in an utterance rather than being attached just to one.

1. Study the file **14_happen.doc**. Can you tell whether the "happening" is regarded as a good thing, a bad thing, or in between, neutral? Consider each instance in turn and try to identify the overall impression you get. Give an indication of your confidence in your judgement, because in some of these instances there is hardly enough cotext to be sure. Keep a note of any words or phrases that help to indicate this aspect of the meaning.

2. The word <u>happen</u> is usually thought to be of neutral meaning. The *Concise Oxford Dictionary* defines it as:

   "come to pass (by chance or otherwise)"

After examining this evidence, would you agree?

3. A number of instances contain expressions of doubt or uncertainty, for example in no. 3 <u>I've no idea</u> expresses doubt and the clause introduced by <u>what</u> is a device for being inexplicit. Look again at each instance and identify words and phrases that indicate uncertainty or vagueness about what is to happen, or its opposite – confidence, certainty and clarity. Where the "happening" has taken place, note any verbal indications of this. Ignore nos. 22 and 24, which are instances of <u>happen to be</u>.

4. How closely does the distinction between doubt and certainty fit the distinction made in §2 between good and bad expectations?

5. Now summarise the basic orientation of the word <u>happen</u>, listing the main criteria that could be used to determine whether a new instance was neutral or tending towards one of the poles. How would you describe the semantic prosody of <u>happen</u> and the words round about it?

6. The two instances of <u>happen to be</u> were removed from the others on the assumption that they showed a separate meaningful pattern. Look first at the file **14_happento.doc**. Here are twelve instances of the phrase. Decide how they fit into the three-point classification good–neutral–bad.

7. The word <u>to</u> makes two rather different structures in English, depending on what follows it. If the next word, or the headword of the next element of structure, is a verb, it forms the infinitive; if it is a noun, it forms a preposi-tional phrase. Go through the file and add this part-of-speech information. How does it correlate with the results of §6?

8. Now look at the file **14_happentobe.doc** and classify it as in §5. Sum-marise the form–meaning relationships of <u>happen</u>, etc., in these two files, and relate the semantic prosody of these phrases to the position stated in your answer to §6.

9. Here is a footnote concerning the likely frequency of words and phrases: <u>happen</u> occurs 41484 times in the Bank of English, <u>happen to</u> occurs 7173 times, and <u>happen to be</u> occurs 1207 times; 7173 is 17% of 41484, and 1207 is 17% of 7173. Can you guess from these figures some relationship be-tween the number of words in a phrase and the number of times the phrase occurs?

Datafile 14_happen.doc

1	no doubt that a breakaway will	happen	. New-look Derby;
2	as a fluke,' we say. 'It couldn't	happen	again.' The cheers ringing in our
3	Balmain. 'I've no idea what will	happen	at the end of the season,' he
4	He thought it was what I wanted to	happen	, but he couldn't have been more wrong
5	be immense. That nightmare may never	happen	. But I wouldn't bet on it. Maybe it'
6	questions about what might	happen	. But, as captain, I back every
7	That's going – No – to	happen	. Erm can you describe sort of
8	few days, but they believe it will	happen	eventually. The release of Mr
9	out any compensation should it	happen	. Given that Connolly can put only
10	page 90 into 'This isn't supposed to	happen	. I've spent nine years structuring
11	I will die. I do not know what will	happen	. I appeal to the American
12	reluctantly asked what would	happen	if the North Vietnamese did not in
13	examples – is what would	happen	if we rid ourselves of that fearful
14	to the pound, great things can also	happen	in Greece without breaking the
15	hooligans. The miracle didn't	happen	. Instead, he cavorted loudly in the
16	While you're waiting for this to	happen	, just surf the Net instead. Whether
17	so rich that recanalization may well	happen	. Just as important is the fact that
18	amazed tragedies like this do not	happen	more often. Mrs LAURA HOLDEN
19	is something seismic starting to	happen	, something as important as the
20	the town, and nobody knows what will	happen	then. Adams: Why do you think
21	Committee and nothing's going to	happen	there for a while. Instead of
22	in which the abuse can occur. It can	happen	to children at any age, from birth
23	distance. It is no fun at all if you	happen	to be nearby. If the star that goes
24	divides the Tory part is what's to	happen	to our border controls after
25	couple in the deodorant ad who just	happen	to be frolicking naked in the

Datafile 14_happento.doc

1	are there and what is going to	happen to	them, the better they will
2	of the world, waiting for things to	happen to	other people. He was part of the
3	benefits. And all these things	happen to	coincide with a major
4	s a little mud, anyway? It could	happen to	anybody. How's your back, by the
5	so many more people that that could	happen to	if you could just get them in
6	you have to be cruel to be kind. I	happen to	feel Enzo has taken Joe as far
7	of people. What to – what's going to	happen to	those people? Cooper: Kubeka
8	you know exactly what was going to	happen to	you Yeah. Yeah.
9	it was possible that this could	happen to	me.' You never thought –
10	others; Do not wish bad things to	happen to	others; Do not steal; It's a
11	there is no indication of what will	happen to	its 320 branches. There is a
12	are we portrayed as screwed up if we	happen to	sleep around asks a well-

Datafile 14_happentobe.doc

1	religion are we going to put? I	happen to be	a Catholic. I don't think
2	That this hapless fellow should	happen to be	a private detective called –
3	admittedly, film-makers who just	happen to be	British); the socialist
4	of me that are there. And if they	happen to be	called feminine by some
5	So that's . . . two	happen to be	in the middle of the range.
6	on. Some of its boldest moments also	happen to be	its most simple ones. There
7	but it all depends on what it is you	happen to be	kissing. Cheeks are fine, but
8	present age may be. Many of them	happen to be	more entertaining than the
9	non-political civil servants who	happen to be	popular with their only real
10	appearing to preach, and they	happen to be	those that Middle Americans
11	dare mention two years on. They also	happen to be	very good, heaping layers of
12	on alienation. The characters just	happen to be	young people who live in

Task 14

Key

1. The kind of expectation about what is going to happen is shown in the following table.

Expectation	No.	Expression
good – definitely	2	cheers
	13	rid ourselves of
	14	great
	19	seismic
good – probably	8	release, eventually
	16	waiting
neutral	21	nothing, for a while
	23	to be
	25	to be
bad – probably	1	breakaway
	3	
	6	questions
	7	No (interjected)
	17	
	24	
bad – definitely	4	wrong
	5	nightmare
	9	compensation
	10	supposed to
	11	die
	12	reluctantly
	15	miracle
	18	tragedies
	20	
	22	abuse

If there is a clear expression of waiting patiently for something to happen, then it is unlikely to be bad (or else, presumably, something would be done to avert it). This is the reason for the allocation of nos. 8 and 16 to "probably good" and no. 21 to "neutral".

2. Certainly not. If we examine the breakdown above, it seems as if <u>happen to be</u> is a separate meaningful unit from the other instances, and we will examine it later. Meanwhile we can remove the two instances of it, giving the following breakdown:

definitely good	4
probably good	2
neutral	1
probably bad	6
definitely bad	<u>10</u>
	<u>23</u>

The weight of the numbers is heavily towards the "bad" end – 70% are bad. Of those classified as "probably bad", some are only in doubt because of the short cotext; if expanded it becomes obvious that what happens is bad. For example in a wider cotext of no. 17, it becomes obvious that "recanalization" is undesirable, although in other uses it may be highly approved of. So we can say that there is a strong tendency for <u>happen</u> to set up an expectation that what happens/will happen, etc., is something unfortunate. This is an aspect of PROSPECTION; we encounter an occurrence of <u>happen</u> and we make an initial assumption that it prospects an unfortunate event. If a word like <u>tragedy</u> or <u>nightmare</u> is in the subject and comes in front of <u>happened</u>, then our assumption is already made by those words, and is merely confirmed; if a phrase like <u>great things</u> appears, it conflicts with the expectations of <u>happen</u> and normally cancels the "unfortunate" meaning orientation.

3. Doubt expressed:

No.	Expression	Modal	Conjunction
3	I've no idea	will	what
4	He thought . . . but		what
5		may	
6	questions	might	what
7	No (interposed)		
9		should (initial)	
11	I do not know	will	what
12	asked	would	what if
13		would	what if
17		may well	
20	nobody knows	will	what
24		's to	what

Certainty or near certainty expressed:

No.	Expression	Modal	Conjunction
1	no doubt	will	
2		couldn't	
8	believe . . . eventually	will	
14		can	
16	waiting		
19	starting to		
21	nothing	's going to	
22		can	

Already determined:

No.	Expression	Reason
10	This	refers to ongoing "happening"
15	didn't	factual statement in the past
18	like this	refers to ongoing "happening"

Notes

- <u>may well</u> is less doubtful than just <u>may</u>.
- <u>will</u> on its own supports certainty (1, 8) but this orientation is cancelled out by a clause beginning with <u>what</u> (3, 11, 20).

4.

	On the doubt side	On the certainty side
On the bad side	3, 4, 5, 6, 7, 9, 11, 12, 17, 20, 24 total **11**	1, 22 total **2**
On the good side	13 total **1**	2, 8, 14, 16, 19 total **5**

Number 21 is neutral and on the certain side; nos. 10, 15, 18, 23 and 25 are not included.

Comment

There is clearly a good correlation between the two criteria. Of the 19 instances analysed, in 16 cases if the event is on the bad side it is also doubtful and if it is on the good side it is close to certain. The three instances that do not correlate are discussed individually below.

Cases for comment

- Number 1. The word breakaway is the reason for this instance being classified as bad; a group of people – here football clubs – is threatening the established order. But it is bad only from one perspective, and from another (e.g. reform) it could be considered very good. So it is only marginally on the bad side, not as strong as nightmare (no. 5), tragedies (no. 18) or abuse (no. 22).
- Number 22. The word abuse makes it quite clear that these are bad events, and while can is not a strongly certain modal, in this instance it is used an alternative to the simple present tense (like "I can hear you", which is preferred in English to "I hear you"). The writing stance is very general, taking a global view of child abuse and not a single incident.
- Number 13. This is the only real exception to the correlation. As shown in the concordance it is rather difficult to classify, because the phrasing – what would happen – normally signals foreboding, and yet rid ourselves and fearful make it clear that the hope is for a good outcome. Here is a longer cotext for this instance:

> I will draw on a number of ethnographic examples – is what would happen if we rid ourselves of that fearful symmetry of loss and redemption

This is not easy to interpret, and we may well conclude that the author has some concern over the outcome, even though he or she apparently approves of the steps being taken to achieve it.

5. The main orientation of happen is the prospection of an unfortunate event happening; this often goes with expressions of doubt and vagueness. Occasionally the word presages the opposite – a desirable event – and in such cases there are often expressions of certainty along with it. If it is clear that there is a period of waiting for the event to happen, it is very unlikely that the event is expected to be unfortunate. Very occasionally the evaluation of the event appears to be neutral.

6 and 7.

	Good	Neutral	Bad
Noun	5		1, 2, 4, 7, 8, 9, 10, 11
Verb		3, 6, 12	

Comment

The fit is perfect. <u>happen to</u> is most often followed by a noun, and there it conforms to the pattern of <u>happen</u>. Eight of the instances here are of the "bad" meaning, but there is one of the "good" to remind us that this is also occasionally possible. Where <u>to</u> is acting as an infinitive marker rather than a preposition, all the instances are neutral.

8. All the instances are neutral. So it is not so much the selection of "<u>be</u>" as the verb, but the selection of a verb rather than a noun that creates the distinction in meaning. We can summarise the position by saying that there is a phrase in English <u>happen</u> + <u>to</u>-infinitive which is separate from <u>happen</u>. It is separate because it takes up a neutral position with respect to what is or may happen or has happened, whereas, as we have seen, <u>happen</u> in any other structure tends to suggest a bad event, though occasionally a good one.

(A little note here about the file **14_happentobe. doc**. I get the overall impression that this meaning is not quite neutral, but that it can be a little ironic or aggressive. The phrase makes explicit that people involved in an event have no responsibility for what happens to be the case, and so when the next word is <u>kissing</u> (no. 7) that is a little ironic since normally kissing involves a serious choice of partner. In no. 3 there is a suggestion that it is not a coincidence that the film-makers are British. This point would have to be researched more thoroughly, but since I am convinced that language is rarely neutral, the faint suggestion of an edge even to this meaning is reassuring.)

9. The notion of a word choice being independent of other word choices is very strong, and it predicts that the likelihood of any two words occurring together is the product of the chances of each being in its position; so if two common words each occur on average once in every 500 words of text, the chances of them being next to each other is roughly 1:250,000. For most pairs of words the chances are extremely low. On the other hand, the notion of CO-SELECTION, the simultaneous choice of more than one word at a time, works in the opposite direction, increasing the chances of certain pairs dramatically. As a result we may observe that a two-word phrase, while not as rare as the arithmetical predictions would have it, is still not nearly as common as the words that make it up, and a three-word phrase is even less common. The figures here suggest that each extra word reduces the number of instances by 83%; this actual number is not important, and the regularity of the reduction in this example is neater than most, but it indicates the scale of reduction. So while <u>happen to be</u> is a phrase that is felt by native speakers to be quite normal and available, it is a lot less common than <u>happen to</u> and a great deal less common than just <u>happen</u>.

LEVEL 4

Task 15

Closely related meanings

A dictionary isolates one word at a time and follows a very basic assumption that each word carries or creates meaning by itself. A speaker or writer chooses the word, and the meaning arrives in the text. From this perspective there are many cases where one word appears to produce different meanings on different occasions.

The different meanings of a word may be a matter of historical accident, where words that used to look and sound quite different have fallen together in their physical or phonetic shape. A well-known example is "bear", which has two main meanings – a noun meaning a large hairy animal, and a verb meaning to carry. Sometimes the meanings are quite clearly related, and we call one of them LITERAL, and the other FIGURATIVE or METAPHORICAL; see Section 4 and Section 12 for details of these different kinds of meaning.

Sometimes, however, a word can have several meanings that are closely related and yet quite distinct; the differences are not of the literal/figurative type. In these cases we must look closely at the surrounding COTEXT to understand how we can identify in each case the relevant meaning. In this section we will examine the verb manage.

The aim of this task is to work out (a) how many meanings the verb manage has, and (b) how the differences are signalled in the texts. In Section 1 we began by asking question (a), but here we will make no assumptions about the number of meanings, but start with the assumption that there will be textual clues to the meanings, and so we start by examining the cotexts of manage.

1. Look at the file **15_manage1.doc**, and particularly at the words that immediately follow manage. Make a list of those which are repeated.

2. Look more closely at the instances where to follows manage.
   (a) When is it the infinitive marker, and when is it the preposition?
   (b) Does manage have a similar meaning in each instance?
   (c) Provide a word or phrase of similar meaning.

3. Now look at the instances where manage is immediately followed by it.
   (a) Do you think that it refers to a preceding noun phrase, or to something else, or is it used "absolutely", without a specific reference?
   (b) Does manage have a similar meaning in each instance?
   (c) Provide a word or phrase of similar meaning.
   (d) Is it close to the meaning of the instances in §2 above?

4. Now look at the instances followed by the.
   (a) Does the begin an object for manage?
   (b) Are the instances similar in meaning to each other?
   (c) Provide a word or phrase that paraphrases this meaning.

5. Ask the same questions about the two instances followed by this.

6. Ask the same questions about the two instances followed by you.

7. Ask the same questions about the two instances followed by she.

8. We have now identified three main meanings of the verb "manage", as follows:

A. accomplish
B. organise
C. cope

Meaning A carries the sense of "with difficulty", "overcoming problems".
Meaning B carries the sense of continuity rather than achieving a specific objective.
Meaning C suggests that the subject of the verb is thought to be close to desperate.

Meaning A was found when manage was followed by a "to" infinitive or the object it.
Meaning B was found when manage was followed by a direct object starting with the.
Meaning C was found when manage had no object.

Now look at the remaining instances and see how far they follow this classification of meaning, and how the structural framework may have to be extended.

9. The file **15_manageit.doc** contains 20 instances of manage immediately followed by it. It will allow us to explore a little more deeply how a transitive use of manage can create the meaning "accomplish". Consider each instance and try to decide if the dominant meaning is close to "accomplish" or to "organise"; then relate your decisions to the referents of it. I have included sufficient cotext for the antecedent of it to be determined, or summarised more distant references.

10. Return to the original data file **15_manage1.doc**, and look more widely at the choice of cotexts. Are there any other choices which appear to be co-ordinated with the meanings?

11. Now turn to the file **15_manage2.doc**. Apply to each instance in turn the dual criteria of meaning and transitivity that we have built up in this section. Be ready to divide Meaning B into two subtypes as follows:

- B1: the original meaning of taking day-to-day charge of a business, an institution or some part of it and making it function efficiently on a continuing basis.
- B2: controlling and coping with problems of a more personal or individual nature, usually outside the institutional framework, e.g. managing stress.

Note the following information which lies outside the short cotexts given:

No. 8:   it is a crisis.
No. 11: the bashing is given by the one guy, not received. This is an unusual instance which will be discussed in the Comments.
No. 14: the condition is a disease.
No. 15: the context here is of business.
No. 23: them are schoolchildren.

12. Add up the number of instances of each of the patterns A, B and C, keeping the division B1 and B2 as a secondary distinction. Compare the dual classification that you have worked out from the evidence here with the entries for manage in several dictionaries, to see (a) how similar the sense categories are, and (b) how far the structural patterns are associated with the meanings.

Datafile 15_manage1.doc

1   against his cheek You'll manage , she said softly. When
2   night. Erm I can't manage . You can't manage? No.
3   on her arms can you manage you're going to
4   the debts of of the companies they manage ? The sums in the Maxwell case
5   and looks back on his failure to manage affairs of state properly", and
6   come a time when they can no longer manage alone. People who are ill or
7   an excellent songster and easy to manage . As the mainstay of its diet it
8   that it could help some women to manage entirely without pain-relieving
9   beyond the ability of either side to manage it would override any benefit an
10 teenage unemployment, Mary might yet manage it. Sophronia Tibbles
11 as stars-in-waiting. Some manage it. Some fail miserably. And some
12 missing, I just don't think they'll manage it.
13 guide by Jeremy Rosenblatt on how to manage it without the expense of a lawyer.
14 answer yet as to how we're going to manage our way through it and out of it
15 baby home until she's sure he can manage . She'll expect him to be thriving,
16 for information and registration. Manage Stress to Live Longer and Healthier
17 said yesterday, 'and no one can manage such a thing One indication
18 harming anyone." How do you manage that, then? We just shut out
19 talk about business plans, how to manage the factories financially, in fact,
20 major games who can manage scrums, manage the line-outs and, above all,
21 the company wants to continue to manage the complex because of the center's
22 although it engages P & O Catering to manage the catering David has no doubt
23 of his peers because he learned to manage their opinions or think too highly
24 many different specializations they manage . This is most clearly seen in guano
25 the republic's political life. They manage this despite Serbia's nosediving
26 know nor care How did you manage to get here, then I filched
27 FRANKL: For those who do manage to get arrested, a brief spell in
28 cabinet), and if the Americans manage to breed the best basketball
29 cut back, the group should still manage to lift profits from Pounds 215m to
30 Mr Gladstone, as long ago as 1876, manage to rouse a large number of the
31 to have him arrested, Keneally does manage to avoid some of the flak. A cousin
32 important to us both. We could never manage without them and we did not intend

Datafile 15_manageit.doc

1. They almost meet one day when Veronique is on a coach tour of Polish towns but they don't quite **manage it**

2. But only 2 per cent over the age of 66 could manage sex twice a week, and none of those over 56 could **manage it** more than three times a week

3. Start gradually, if you're not used to it, 5–10 minutes brisk walking and work up to half an hour 3–4 times a week – everyday if you can **manage it**.

4. The Socialists have promised labour reform for years. They did not **manage it** when they had a majority; now they are weaker.

5. The Budget coverage you read on Wednesday morning was as controled as the Government could **manage it**.

6. I am trying to help you, but I cannot **manage it** without your thoughts.

7. (unused farmland) Are we simply going to say 'This is preserved.' If we are, how are we going to **manage it**? How are we going to pay for this preservation?

8. they've tried to have sex and couldn't **manage it**.

9. (a tolerant society) accepting diversity and welcoming difference," she said. "This will be one of the big challenges of the next number of years." She warned: "How we **manage it** now will decide whether or not we have problems in the future."

10. (writing a play scene) I don't suppose I knew then that I would be able to do it, that I'd be able to **manage it**.

11. (using spreadsheets and) Querymaster and whatever else but by and large I don't have the need to do it. Right. I'm quite a . . . Are y . . . Could **manage it** if I had to I think

12. When we set up <Grange> House we thought – I never thought that someone like myself could **manage it**. We – I – was very clear at the time that it would be managed by a nurse.

13. In due course they will be packed up and stored, or sent to Tresillian. This was the best way we could **manage it**

14. He flushed. "Mother is – over-protective. She never let me go away to school. How did you **manage it**?" "She wanted me out of her life."

15. In any case, acknowledging the awesome power and wisdom of God, the question is not "How could He **manage it** in just six days?", but rather "Why did it take Him so long?"

16. (Confucius becoming happy) If it takes seventy years for a very wise man how long is it going to take for an ordinary man? He is never going to **manage it**.

17. (politician after defeat) 'I have survived it, there is more to life than the politics. Though my first preference is to go back, if I don't **manage it**,

18. Hamleys is the biggest seller of fireworks in the world and sells them throughout the year. They have to be so organised to **manage it** legally and they are very practiced with it.

19. You can buy a property outside the Arla scheme and **manage it** yourself

20. to help someone short of money, and it would be worth taking on a temporary job to finance the course. Ask your parents for help, if they can **manage it**.

Datafile 15_manage2.doc

1	venture deal with Agip of Italy to	manage	18 hotels. George Soros,
2	Julie Britton, a housewife, could	manage	.
3	pace, but was finally just able to	manage	a top 20 placing. Few people
4	her mouth doesn't look big enough to	manage	an olive, let alone a stick of
5	this, local people could better	manage	both the diminishing woodlands
6	position. Harding could only	manage	eighth place when she finally
7	children in this age group who can't	manage	even three-letter words, has risen
8	in the Third World and agreed to	manage	it. In the last two weeks, he
9	years ago I've only ever wanted to	manage	Leonard Cohen and the Waterboys and
10	that it's wrong to ask a manager to	manage	my budget Mm. because I
11	s a lot of bashing for one guy to	manage	; drop them both in their
12	is in jeopardy." Prime will	manage	Ramada's domestic franchise system,
13	someone up in a club. I always	manage	somehow, but it can be really hard
14	it is far preferable to try to	manage	the condition without resorting to
15	Clearly, when an organization has to	manage	the transition from one stage to
16	explained. My husband gave me cash to	manage	the household, but none of it was
17	to convince people that he can	manage	the change. Edwards: All right
18	It is a blow to the way in which we	manage	the NHS. I think the government,
19	way for the world to learn how to	manage	the post-cold war era
20	although it engages P&O Catering to	manage	the catering. David has no doubt
21	was sent down from Springwood to	manage	their little household and
22	for most NHS patients) the chance to	manage	their own budgets. This notion of
23	their quality world. Unless we can	manage	them so that many more are
24	is it such a best-seller? How did he	manage	to create this extraordinary
25	rare and fascinating occasions they	manage	to avoid it. Theories of
26	He did, but he couldn't quite	manage	to brush his teeth But you
27	meets Loving Spoonful! This they	manage	to spit out in what seems like less
28	Singaporeans still prefer to (and	manage	to) find partners all by
29	great to see him man	manage	to be able to afford to get it that'
30	are bought. Well how do they	manage	to get that sort of I don't
31	of how how we	manage	to move on from the very beginning
32	performances from the three lads who	manage	to convey a great feeling of

Task 15

Key

1. to   6
   it   5
   the   5
   she   2
   this   2
   you   2

2. (a) They are all the infinitive marker.
   (b) Yes.
   (c) "accomplish with difficulty", "contrive".

Note that no. 27 has ironic meaning. We expect in this usage that what follows
to is a desirable goal, whereas getting arrested is not usually regarded as
desirable. By making the ironic assumption that getting arrested is desirable,
the instance now fits in with the rest.

3. (a) The cotexts are too small to be certain, but I would guess that there is
       no noun antecedent of any of these instances of it. More likely there
       will be a clause.
   (b) Yes.
   (c) "accomplish with difficulty".
   (d) The meaning is very similar to §2.

4. (a) Yes.
   (b) Yes.
   (c) "organise in continuity" – control and take responsibility for an institu-
       tion or process or behaviour, over a period of time.

5. The two cases are quite different. In no. 24 This starts a new sentence and
plays no structural role with respect to manage. The verb is in a relative clause
where the nearest expression of the object is the phrase that finishes many
different specializations. This phrase probably begins with "the", and the meaning fits in with the other instances of the in §4.
   In no. 25 the word this is the object, and its meaning fits with the instances
of it in §3.

6. (a) No. In both cases the word you begins a new clause or sentence.
   (b) Yes – the meaning of manage is similar in both cases.
   (c) "cope".

7. (a) In both instances <u>she</u> begins a new clause, and <u>manage</u> has no object.
   (b) Yes.
   (c) "cope".

8.

No.	Structural status	Model	Meaning type	Class
1	intransitive	2 etc.	cope	C
4	quasi-transitive in relative clause	24	organise	B
5	transitive; institutional object	19 etc.	organise	B
6	intransitive	2 etc.	cope	C
7	hidden passive – see note		organise	B
8	intransitive – see note		cope/organise	C/B
14	transitive; "dummy" object		accomplish	A
16	transitive; emotional object		organise/cope with	B
17	transitive; object propositional reference	10 etc.	accomplish	A
18	transitive; object propositional reference	10 etc.	accomplish	A
23	transitive; emotional object	16	organise/cope with	B
32	intransitive	2 etc.	cope	C

Notes

Meaning A

The essence of this meaning is that someone reaches a goal with difficulty; it occurs in transitive structures where the object is a pronoun that normally refers to a clause, rather than a noun group. The object is extended here in two phrases, <u>our way</u> and <u>such a thing</u>. Note that the first of these is almost redundant semantically, and so is mainly useful as a "transitiser"; in the second the object is extremely vague and almost certainly refers back to a clause in the preceding text.

Meaning B

The typical meaning here is of someone who takes day-to-day charge of an institution and makes it function efficiently – the work of a manager. The object is usually a business or an office, and we found this meaning principally in front of <u>the</u>. Numbers 4 and 5 are similar instances.

In no. 7 we find an active intransitive structure, and yet it has a passive meaning, because it is the songster that is going to be managed. Chomsky drew attention to this meaning in a famous contrast between "John is eager to please" and "John is easy to please" (Syntactic Structures 1957). In the first, John is eager to please someone else, and in the second, someone or something pleases John with ease.

In no. 16 there is an extension of meaning B into the area of personal emotions and problems. The verb is transitive, so the "organise" meaning is dominant, but because the object expresses something very personal, such as stress, opinions or grief, the idea of coping is not far below the surface. I have glossed the meaning as "organise/cope <u>with</u>" to make the point that meaning emphasises continuity, and that there is an object in the clause.

Number 23 is very similar to no.16.

Meaning C

Of the four intransitive uses of <u>manage</u>, three are of the "cope" meaning. In no. 8 there is a mixed pattern of meaning; in childbirth the mother is both coping and organising something, and it is difficult to determine in the abstract which idea might be dominant. But the verb <u>manage</u> is used intransitively, which suggests that the "cope" meaning is uppermost and the "organise" meaning is secondary. We must avoid creating problems for ourselves here – in real-life communication we do not have the luxury of analysis.

Coping is also an element of nos. 16 and 23, where it is again mixed with "organise", but with secondary weight.

Summary

The fit between the intransitive use of <u>manage</u> and the meaning of "cope" is fairly clear.

The fit between the occurrence of a noun group as object of <u>manage</u> and the meaning of "organise" is also good, with different shades of meaning according to whether the object is an institution or a personal emotion. Occasionally there is a noun object which refers to neither of these things, but vaguely back to a proposition, and these instances fit better with the meaning "accomplish".

This meaning is clear when <u>manage</u> is followed by a "to" infinitive, but it also arises with certain kinds of transitive clause; most instances of <u>it</u> as object create this meaning, and the vague phrases noted above. The criterion for distinguishing between "organise" and "accomplish" in transitive uses of <u>manage</u> is the nature of the object; if it refers to a proposition expressing an activity then the meaning is "accomplish", while if it is a conventional noun group, the meaning is "organise".

9. The meaning is "accomplish" in all the instances except four – nos. 7, 9, 12 and 19, where the meaning is "organise". In no. 9 the object <u>it</u> refers to society; perhaps there is a little ambiguity here, but for me it is clearly "organise". In the other three instances <u>it</u> refers to a piece of real estate – farmland or buildings – which are solid, institutional things – "organise" again.

In most of the others the referent of <u>it</u> can be seen as a proposition; in no. 1, for example, it is "they meet", in no. 2 it is "manage sex", in no. 3 it is "walking briskly for half-an-hour a day", in no. 4 it is "reform labour", in no. 5 it is "the Government controls the budget". Numbers 2 and 8 show euphemism in the phrases <u>manage sex</u> and <u>have sex</u>, where "sex" means sexual intercourse.

10. Meaning C, and the intransitive use of <u>manage</u>, appear to be co-ordinated with a choice of the modal verbs <u>can, could</u>. Out of eight instances of this

pattern, five have the modal, and it occurs only twice elsewhere, in nos. 17 and 20.

11.

No.	Type	Structure	Wording	Notes
1	B1	transitive	hotels	institutional
2	C	intransitive		
3	A	transitive	a top 20 placing	object = a rating
4	A	transitive	an olive	see comments below
5	B1	transitive	woodlands	institutional
6	A	transitive	eighth place	object = a rating (compare 3)
7	A	transitive	three-letter words	see comments below
8	B2	transitive	it	crisis management
9	B1	transitive	Leonard Cohen	a pop star = a business
10	B1	transitive	my budget	institutional
11	A	transitive	a lot of bashing	see comments below
12	B1	transitive	. . . franchise system	institutional
13	C	intransitive		
14	B2	transitive	the condition	personal problem
15	B2	transitive	the transition	see comments below
16	B1	transitive	the household	domestic-institutional
17	B2	transitive	the change	see comments below
18	B1	transitive	the NHS	institutional
19	B2	transitive	the post-cold war era	see comments below
20	B1	transitive	the catering	institutional
21	B1	transitive	their little household	institutional
22	B1	transitive	their own budgets	institutional
23	B2	transitive	them	individual – see comments
24	A	to-infinitive		
25	A	to-infinitive		
26	A	to-infinitive		
27	A	to-infinitive		
28	A	to-infinitive		
29	A	to-infinitive		
30	A	to-infinitive		
31	A	to-infinitive		
32	A	to-infinitive		

Comments

There are several instances of Meaning A with an object, and we will have to recognise a greater variety of objects than before. Numbers 3 and 6 introduce as object a rating in a competition. The meaning is of accomplishing with effort, overcoming problems, and so is an A. Such objects are fairly distinct from the B-type objects. In no. 4 the meaning is again principally A, but since the activity referred to is eating an olive, which would not normally be considered a great achievement, there is a touch of irony in this instance. In no. 7, a further kind of object is found, in this case an educational target, and it seems that almost any noun can be the object of <u>manage</u>; it is a productive structure and the reader/listener has to interpret the meaning, usually by imagining an appropriate verb, such as "eating" an olive or "spelling" three-letter words.

We first encountered Meaning A where <u>manage</u> was followed by structure introduced by a "to" infinitive, expressing an accomplishment. Numbers 24–32 are uncomplicated instances of this pattern. Then we found that the object <u>it</u> frequently referred back to such an expression, and Meaning A was appropriate. In these further examples it seems that although the grammatical object is a noun group, it is interpreted as an accomplishment. So <u>manage eighth place</u> is interpreted as "manage to achieve eighth place".

Number 11 is very unusual; it refers to photographs of a nasty double murder, and the question of whether the murder could have been committed by one person alone. So the closest meaning is again A, and the quasi-object <u>a lot of bashing</u> can be interpreted as kind of accomplishment.

In Meaning B, the distinction between B1 and B2 holds up but needs some further extension and explanation. The original distinction was that the object of a B2 pattern was some personal or individual problem; the sense of handling a situation in continuity was common to both B1 and B2. Number 14 adds disease to the range of problems. But we also find B2 patterns in the institutional area, concerning the management of change, in nos. 15 and 17; so if you manage a company that is B1, keeping it working efficiently, and if you manage it through a transition, you also manage the transition, which is B2.

B2 is also found in the handling of general political situations such as the post-cold war era (no. 19).

Number 23 is particularly tricky because it talks about managing school-children in the sense of getting them to choose scientific subjects. From one perspective it could be B1, in that school administrators manage schoolchildren (but this <u>we</u> is very general and refers to society as a whole); if it is an instance of B2 it is close to the meaning of "manipulate".

12. Totals:

Meaning A: 28
Meaning B: 27 of which B1: 18, B2: 9 (approximately)
Meaning C: 9

No key for dictionary enquiries.

Task 16

One and one is not exactly two

There are in English a large number of phrases which occur in fairly regular patterns. In the case of each phrase there is a considerable amount of variation but enough similarity for the phrases to be seen as instances of the same meaning. We tend to call them idioms if there is something unusual about the meaning – for example if the meaning cannot be worked out from the normal meanings of the individual words. But the meaning is not necessarily remarkable – quite often a regular pattern can be observed where all the words have approximately their normal meanings. This exercise concerns an example of a regular phrase, and after studying its form and range we shall return to think about the reason why it occurs in such a regular form, and if there is anything special about the meaning.

1. Study the concordance for true feelings held in the datafile **16_truefeelings1.doc**. Look first at the word immediately to the left and list the words that occur at least twice in that position in order of their frequency.

2. What is the commonest word class? What is the commonest word that is *not* a member of that word class? Look at the cotext to the right of each of the instances of this word, and suggest how these instances can be related to the commonest word class.

3. Now look at the next word to the left of the "possession" marker. Organise the words there into word-classes, and note any repeated items. What kind of meaning do you associate with the words in the commonest word-class?

4. Of the verbs to do with expressing things, you may detect contrasting meanings. Attempt a classification of these verbs, and then compose a generalisation that covers around two-thirds of them.

5. Look to the left of the verbs in the "reveal" class. Are you aware of any recurrent strand of meaning among at least some of them? At this distance from the invariable part of the phrase it is unlikely that you will find many words repeated exactly, but the similarity in meaning should come through. Unfortunately in some instances the evidence is too far away from the centre of the phrase that it lies beyond the quoted line; however, there is often at least a clue at the beginning or end of the line, so make guesses where there is no hard evidence.

6. Make a summary of the structure and meaning of the unit of meaning that has as its core true feelings.

7. When you are fairly sure that you have captured the meaningful patterns of your first set of examples, go to **16_truefeelings2.doc** and check how far your description is adequate for this new set of instances. See if you can add to the word-classes and means of expression, and perhaps note some new variations. (You probably noticed that the first datafile was just a portion of a concordance, taken from the middle. This second datafile is the rest of the concordance, the portions before and after the first set. Together they make up a sample of 84 instances.)

Datafile 16_truefeelings1.doc

1	more accustomed to denying our	true feelings , avoiding reflection and self-
2	We try to communicate our	true feelings to those around us, and are told
3	the ability to express our	true feelings and creativity because we are
4	we appease others, deny our	true feelings , and conform. I suspected the
5	more of us in there, of our	true feelings , rather than just ranting on about
6	Cancerian lover to reveal	true feelings so trust and love can blossom. You
7	abandonment. For to have one's	true feelings , perceptions, and thoughts negated
8	Arab summit representing the	true feelings of all Arabs, some of whom had
9	account of history and the	true feelings of people. Q: How would you propose
10	shows no regard for the	true feelings and their needs. The blatant
11	Your month ahead: The	true feelings and emotions of your partner will
12	why?" you may prompt the	true feelings behind the anger to come out and
13	up and soothing down the	true feelings , hopes and demands of an oppressed
14	not the faintest idea of the	true feelings of Julia Somerville, the
15	my patients discover their	true feelings about the different therapies
16	Then they pour out their	true feelings . After emergency surgery to remove
17	from expressing their	true feelings on many aspects of life. Mr
18	people from expressing their	true feelings . 370 BAND THREE DUR: 12 secs. Senior
19	for them to express their	true feelings , and this can come between them
20	will need to communicate their	true feelings to their teams in an environment
21	politicians to tell you their	true feelings about their fellow politicians and
22	but abruptness betrayed their	true feelings . Were they disappointed to have
23	seething, hiding their	true feelings in adolescent petulance? I
24	less open about showing their	true feelings and noticeably less polite than
25	have little regard for their	true feelings about topics they know intimately,
26	the lovers who conceal their	true feelings behind barbed witticisms at each
27	but have now followed their	true feelings . I think one day I too will have
28	it comes to revealing their	true feelings . Why hold back and miss out on so
29	form about their – their	true feelings . And oddly enough, to write
30	they'll disguise their	true feelings So when – generally speaking, if
31	guilty about expressing their	true feelings . They don't want to bore
32	cakes magically flavoured with	true feelings . Taste it and see.
33	you'll be inclined to hide you	true feelings behind a mask of aloofness this
34	you may find that your	true feelings on the matter emerge quite clearly.
35	When you finally admit to your	true feelings I shall hear you say, "I love

Datafile 16_truefeelings2.doc

1	Confused as to the Allies'	true feelings	, Haig commented that 'the
2	touch with their own needs and	true feelings	full stop, being so anxious to
3	incapable of experiencing	true feelings	. And not just as a man, but even
4	moment ago to share his or her	true feelings	with a team. Courageous sharing
5	and loneliness to mask her	true feelings	. As the day passed she
6	her formal policy and her	true feelings	. It is Mrs Thatcher's negative
7	to befriend Alison but her	true feelings	for her were poured out in a hate-
8	for O'Shaughnessy and her	true feelings	of suppressed jealousy were
9	the Princess of Wales show her	true feelings	. The thousands standing
10	He may not want to admit his	true feelings	of ambivalence because he wants to
11	the growing red stain, had his	true feelings	broken free from his dying heart
12	face for signs of his	true feelings	. Did he mean it? Could he really be
13	perhaps giving vent to his	true feelings	about the massacre, General
14	and the other person as to his	true feelings	in the relationship, usually due
15	in his efforts to conceal his	true feelings	. "I'm not ill," she said. "I'm
16	Chaucer, is to disguise his	true feelings	: 'And softe sighed, lest men
17	If they were his	true feelings	. Perhaps he was suffering from a
18	giving an inkling of his	true feelings	? If they were his true
19	and happy hero reveals his	true feelings	for his friend Willie Polhaven
20	charmer will never reveal his	true feelings	; he has to appear hard, macho and
21	I know others were making his	true feelings	perfectly clear. In the end I've
22	to his audience and hiding his	true feelings	behind careful constructions. Even
23	said Taylor was aware of his	true feelings	for Alison, but admitted keeping
24	of his way to make public his	true feelings	about Gower, claimed that under
25	only sounding boards for his	true feelings	are likely to be close female
26	a man who resolutely kept his	true feelings	under wraps, he also manages to
27	Now I had to confront my	true feelings	about my body, another struggle to
28	because I had betrayed my	true feelings	. I picked up the glass and took
29	the people who mattered. My	true feelings	had to be buried, the curtain rung
30	so careful about expressing my	true feelings	and told them things that were
31	myself to acknowledge my	true feelings	maybe because having a
32	when I'm able to reveal my	true feelings	. Can we win? Yes, but we
33	prevents me from expressing my	true feelings	. Ford: But the courts failure to
34	two years to experience my	true feelings	for him, and during that time I
35	communication, and exchange of	true feelings	, and we can be thankful when
36	you do share your	true feelings	. Then you can go on to make sure
37	have been unable to share your	true feelings	with him. As a result, it now
38	be time for you to show your	true feelings	, and stop pretending you're happy
39	dreams can help indicate your	true feelings	at the moment – take heed of them.
40	you were forced to hide your	true feelings	during childhood and became self-
41	you cannot communicate your	true feelings	means you put out stress hormones
42	not be keenly aware of your	true feelings	until later, when you're on your
43	Love. It's hard to express your	true feelings	early in August, but later on all
44	you play games to hide your	true feelings	, nobody every wins. By Lesley
45	problems or insights into your	true feelings	. THE SILVA 'GLASS OF
46	close wants to know your	true feelings	. And things will improve immensely
47	it much easier to express your	true feelings	. You now have benevolent Jupiter
48	response when you express your	true feelings	. Take a good look at your money
49	less rude than explaining your	true feelings	? I think not. Worst of all,

Task 16

Key

1. their	17
the	7
our	5
your	2

2. The commonest word class is the possessive adjective. In total there are 24 instances of these words, and the single instance of *you* seems to be a printing error for *your*. Also in the class is *one's*, making a grand total of 26 out of 35 instances.

The commonest word that is not in the class is *the*. If we look at the words to the right of *the true feelings*, we see that in three of the instances the next word is *of*; two more examples have *of* present but a few words away. One more case – no. 10 – may well be a misprint for *their*. So nearly all of these examples show a structure which is usually regarded as a phrasal alternative to the possessive adjective; this is the definite article before the noun and an *of*-phrase after it.

This adds up to "possession" being a meaning associated with the phrase in all except two of its occurrences. One of these, line 6, seems to be written in note form, and one of the conventions of note form is that a demonstrative such as the possessive can be omitted. So line 6 is not very different from the others; the possessive is simply not made explicit.

The only remaining line, line 32, shows the phrase being used in a reverse metaphorical sense – as if true feelings were a kind of sugary ingredient in a baking mix; that is unusual and idiosyncratic.

It is safe to conclude from this the following.

(a) In all normal circumstances the meaning "possession" is realised in the close vicinity of the phrase in question.
(b) The commonest way in which it is realised is by a possessive adjective immediately in front of the phrase. Of these, the commonest collocate is *their* and the least common is *our*.
(c) The other way in which "possession" is realised is by the definite article in front of the phrase and an *of*-phrase following.

Both of these ways of creating meaning are grammatical, so this pattern can be called a COLLIGATION. Whereas collocation is the co-occurrence of particular words, colligation is the co-occurrence of a grammatical class (such as possessive adjective) or pattern with a word, phrase or another set of grammatical choices.

3. Most of the words are verbs. Repeated verbs are:

express(ing)	5
communicate	2
deny(ing)	2
reveal(ing)	2
hide (hiding)	2

Note that the instance of <u>reveal</u> is in no. 6, where there is no possessive.

Several of the verbs that occur once only have a similar meaning: <u>prompt</u>, <u>discover</u>, <u>betrayed</u>, <u>conceal</u>, <u>followed</u>, <u>disguise</u>, <u>showing</u>, <u>representing</u> and <u>admit to</u>. There is also <u>pour out</u>, <u>tell</u> and <u>find that . . . emerge</u>.

These are mainly words to do with expression, and they show that the choice of <u>true feelings</u> is part of a larger choice. Although <u>true</u> has a similar meaning to "genuine" and <u>feelings</u> is similar to "emotions", when they come together they tend to form the object of a verb of expression. So it sounds unnatural to make up a sentence like "Fred has true feelings for Mary." or "The true feelings of the people were for revenge, so they stormed the jail."

Where the structure of a phrase, as here, shows repeated choices of words with similar meaning (though not necessarily the same words) we call this a SEMANTIC PREFERENCE. In this instance the preference is for words of expression. Here they are also all verbs, which is not necessary in semantic preference but is in fact an instance of colligation; we can also expect to find some instances where the meaning is realised in a noun or an adjective. There is also evidence of collocation in that, as we saw above, several verbs are repeated and the verb "express" itself occurs four times.

Semantic preference is one step more abstract than colligation, which in turn is more abstract then collocation. Collocation deals with the actual words, sometimes LEMMATISED like "express" – which includes <u>expressing</u> as well as <u>express</u>. Colligation groups words and phrases together on grammatical grounds, and semantic preference groups them together on semantic grounds.

4.

"reveal"	"conceal"
communicate	deny
reveal	betrayed
prompt	hide
discover	conceal
express	admit to
showing	disguise
tell	
pour out	
emerge	

The phrase with <u>true feelings</u> is usually the object of a verb to do with expression; while some of these verbs refer positively to expression, even to ease of expression, others highlight reluctance or difficulty of expression.

5. The verbs <u>reveal,</u> <u>prompt</u> and <u>discover</u> suggest that in this phrase expression is not seen as a straightforward matter. Looking carefully at the verbs of "positive" expression, we discover that in almost every case there is a signal of reluctance or difficulty in the expression, though some of the lines quoted are too short to make this clear. In the table below where I have quoted from beyond what it is possible to include in the concordance line, I have put the quote in square brackets. Apologies to the conscientious student – but there are clues like <u>from</u> in nos. 17 and 18.

No.	Verb	Reluctance	Notes
2	communicate	try to	
3	express	ability to	
6	reveal	[patience can help a timid]	phrase is to the left of the line
12	prompt	come out	phrase occurs on the right-hand side
15	discover	[trying to help]	phrase is to the left of the line
16	pour out	see note	see note
17	expressing	[prevented] from	part lost to the left of the line
18	expressing	[stopping people] from	part lost to the left of the line
19	express	[difficult] for them	part lost to the left of the line
20	communicate	need to	
21	tell	[the task of persuading]	phrase is to the left of the line
24	showing	less open	
28	revealing	hold back	phrase occurs on the right-hand side
		[difficult when]	phrase is to the left of the line
31	expressing	guilty	
34	emerge	may find . . . quite clearly	phrasing occurs on both sides of the node

Note on no. 16: the clue is the first word in the line – <u>then</u>. By implication, something occurred which allowed the expression to flow. The passage around this line is obscure and not a little bizarre, linking surgery with psychological states – after an operation to remove a blocked intestine the patient finds a psychological correlate of the unblocking, and is able to talk about his or her emotional problems.

Conclusion

At this point we can say that all the phrases including verbs of expression include an element of reluctance or difficulty. This is called a SEMANTIC PROSODY, because although it is not always obvious it indicates why the phrase with true feelings has been chosen. From this we deduce that English speakers use the phrase with true feelings when they want to give the meaning of reluctance to express deeply felt emotions.

In the case of the verbs which do not share the semantic preference of expression, we note that there is a parallel for the prosody of reluctance; the true feelings are blocked, ignored or otherwise regarded as of little value.

- In no. 7, have is followed, on the right-hand side, by negated.
- In no. 8, the verb is representing, and the wider cotext includes claim and other indications that the representation may not be reliable.
- In no. 9, the verb is takes account of. In both 8 and 9 there is an implication that people's true feelings are obscure and not necessarily what appears on the surface.
- In no. 10, for comes at the end of the phrase show no regard for.
- Number 13 has soothing down.
- Number 25 is like no. 10, where for completes the phrase have little regard for.
- In no. 27, the verb is followed and the clue is but at the beginning of the line; the topic – recovered from the wider cotext – is sexual identity.

The remaining lines do not contain a verb in front of the node true feelings.

- In no. 5, the word us should be highlighted, and stressed heavily when read out, because the following phrase is an explication of the word us. The occurrence of more of indicates some difficulty in bringing out the true feelings.
- In no. 11, the right cotext continues with the verb revealed, implying that your partner's true feelings are at present obscured.
- In no. 29, the word form at the beginning of the line is the end of the phrase in disguised form, showing an adjective carrying the semantic preference and prosody.

From this consideration of each line in the sample concordance, we conclude that there is a semantic prosody of "reluctance" or something like it that applies in almost every instance; the point of using this expression is to create the meaning of reluctance to express true feelings.

6. The phrase that we have been studying, and that has the meaning and function set out at the end of §5, consists of several elements:

- An invariable CORE which consists of the two words true feelings.
- A colligation "possessive" which is realised by a possessive adjective modifying the core in most instances, but in some is replaced by the definite article the followed by an of-phrase on the other side of the core.

- A word or phrase meaning the expression of one's true feelings, usually a verb to the left of the possessive. This is a semantic preference.
- A word or phrase meaning reluctance or difficulty, usually placed to the left of the semantic preference; this is the semantic prosody. In several cases the meaning of the verb puts together "expression" and "reluctance", e.g. in the verb <u>conceal</u>.

7. This account goes through §1–6 again with the new data, in §7.1–7.6.

7.1. Repeated words immediately to the left of *true feelings*:

his	17
your	14
my	8
her	<u>6</u>
	<u>45</u>

7.2 The possessive adjective is the only repeated word class at this position.

7.3 The commonest word-class is again verbs, and most of the verbs have a semantic preference for expression. Repeated verbs are:

express(ing)	5
reveal(s)	3
hide (hiding)	3
share	2

7.4

"reveal"	"conceal"
show	mask
were	admit
reveal	conceal
make . . . clear	disguise
express	hide
share	kept . . . under wraps
show	
indicate	
communicate	
explaining	
acknowledge	

7.5 The table below goes through each line except those of the "conceal" class and presents evidence for the semantic prosody of reluctance/difficulty.

No.	Verb, etc.	Reluctance, etc.	Notes
1	confused	confused	another variety of possessive
2	[lose] touch	lose touch	just beyond the citation
3	experiencing	incapable	
4	share	[struggling]	a small clue in <u>courageous</u>
6	[conflict between]	conflict	formal policy = outward show
7	poured out	[pretended] to befriend . . . but . . . hate-[filled diary]	the clues in <u>befriend . . . but . . . hate</u> are fairly strong
8	[revealed]	suppressed	
9	show	[make]	just beyond the citation
11	had . . . broken free	had . . . broken free	a formal variant of an "if"-clause
12	signs	Did he mean it?	
13	giving vent to	[not in quoted line]	release of emotion after public concealment
14	as to	[deceive]	
17	were	If . . . suffering	. . . from a [mental illness]
18	giving	an inkling	[without] giving
19	reveals		concealed homosexual relationship
20	reveal	will never	
21	making . . . clear	others	<u>his</u> normally relates back to the subject
23	was aware of	but admitted	
24	make public	went out of his way	effort and difficulty
25	sounding boards	female [friends]	intimacy and secrecy
27	confront	struggle	conflict situation
30	expressing	careful about	
31	acknowledge	[allowed myself to]	[I don't think at this stage I . . .]
32	reveal	able to	
33	expressing	prevents	
34	experience	[it took me two years to . . .]	meeting his real father at age 16
35	exchange		a crisis is the occasion for honesty
36	share	[afraid]	[. . . might happen if you . . .]
37	share	unable	
38	show	stop pretending	
39	indicate	dreams can help	true feelings are subliminal
41	communicate	you cannot	
42	keenly aware	not be . . . until later	
43	express	It's hard to	
45	insights	problems	
46	wants	[someone] close	true feelings obviously hidden
47	express	much easier	
48	express	[a warm] response	[confusions in your emotional affairs are dispelled . . .]
49	explaining	less rude	wider cotext not available

7.6 The investigation of the second concordance shows that the "snapshot" of the first concordance was accurate and reliable. No new categories of meaning have been uncovered, and the only contribution of another 49 instances is to add a few more verbs to the class of "expressing" verbs, and some more ways of expressing the prosody of reluctance or difficulty.

We can therefore set out with some confidence a description of a lexical item in English as follows:

	Semantics		Grammar	Core
PROSODY	reluctance			
PREFERENCE		expression	possession	
COLLIGATION	verb	verb	poss. adj.	
COLLOCATION		hide	his	true feelings
		reveal	their	
		express	your	

Examples	less open about showing	their	true feelings
	you'll be inclined to hide	your	true feelings

There is an implication of word order in the above diagram, reflecting the tendency of the elements of structure to occur in the sequence:

PROSODY PREFERENCE COLLIGATION COLLOCATION CORE

This tendency has been noted in other lexical items – that the more abstract categories come in front of the more concrete ones, so that the invariable physical realisation of the item very often comes at the end. Incidentally this demonstrates fairly graphically how the whole item is a single choice, how in most cases the word feelings has been "chosen" five or more words before it is articulated.

The length of this item in words also shows the limitation of the concordance format, because it takes up half or more of the line, mainly to the left. This has meant that unless the evidence for the more abstract elements of structure is very close, the line is too short to contain it. Once the multi-word lexical item becomes a familiar object of attention the concordances of the future will adapt to its requirements.

Task 17

Common words

The information that a corpus can give you about the usage of a word or phrase is often just a confirmation of what a competent speaker of the language already knows; the corpus adds a lot of useful detail. But also quite often the information is unexpected, and even goes against what authoritative grammars and dictionaries say about the word or phrase in question. Even then the gap between our expectations and the picture given by the corpus can usually be reduced or closed in a way that increases our understanding about the way words work together.

When we are dealing with rather uncommon words, we are likely to learn new things about them anyway; but when we are studying the common words that are used thousands of times a day by everyone, then it is a strange experience to see those words as – in part – strangers. This task invites you to reconsider the information that you have about a very common word in English – the word *place*.

Let us first ask five questions about this word.
A. What is the most common meaning of *place*?
B. When can *place* be missed out with very little damage to the meaning of the sentence it is part of?
C. Can you compose a sentence where it refers directly to a geographical location in the world?
D. Can you think of a usage of it which is rather dismissive?
E. When can it mean where someone lives?

There is no key to these questions – as we go along in the task they will be answered.

1. Examine the datafile **17_place1.doc**. This is a tiny but unbiased selection made by the computer. Find the commonest word that occurs either just before or just after <u>place</u>; put inflected forms of a word together on this occasion.

2. Does this collocation make a different meaning from <u>place</u> on its own? Compare it with the other repeated meanings and work out if it is the commonest in this concordance. Then attempt an answer to Question A.

3. Now look at the datafile **17_place2.doc**. This is another concordance, but it has been constructed in a number of steps. First of all, only occurrences of <u>place</u> as a verb were chosen, and then a collocational profile was made. In order of significance, the noun collocations of <u>place</u> as a verb are:

order, emphasis, value, importance, bet, burden, strain, trust, pressure, bowl, hand(s), restrictions, top, faith, blame, premium, sheet, limits

I wanted to isolate more abstract objects of <u>place</u>, so I rejected the collocates <u>bowl</u>, <u>hands</u> and <u>sheet</u> because these are to do with physical placement. Finally I selected one instance of each of the remaining collocates to give a summary picture of the usage. This is **17_place2.doc**.

Go through each instance and consider whether it is possible to rephrase it, omitting the word <u>place</u> without losing a lot of the meaning. There may be a need for adjustments to maintain grammatical accuracy; the noun object will have to turn into a verb and if <u>place</u> is modified by an adjective then the adjective will have to change into an adverb. After doing this, attempt an answer to Question B.

4. We now turn to issues involved in Question C. In answering Question A many people would assume that this meaning of locational reference was the commonest, so instances should be easy to find. There are some uses of <u>place</u> that do not have locational reference at all, like <u>take place</u>. If we remove these, the others should fulfil the conditions of "referring directly to a geographical location". To make the job easier still, all the non-locational instances have been removed from the datafile **17_place3.doc**. The concordance began as fifty lines chosen without bias by the computer from all the instances in a large corpus, and reduced to 21 by deletion of verb uses, the phrase <u>take place</u>, the result of a competition, e.g. <u>second place</u>, and phrases such as <u>in place</u> and <u>out of place</u>. In addresses and place names <u>Place</u> certainly fulfils the condition of Question C, but instances were also removed because the operation of proper names requires special statements, which are hardly necessary in this study.

Look carefully at each instance in the concordance, and consider where the referent for <u>place</u> is to be found. If it is to be found in the world – directly and not via another word or phrase in the text – then it fulfils the conditions of Question C; if it refers first to another word coming before or after it, then it is a word whose meaning is defined in the text and not in the world. This is a vital distinction, and there are many words in a language which are nearly always text-defined. If someone says <u>Globalisation is the big issue of our time</u>, then you understand <u>issue</u> by referring it to <u>globalisation</u>, and not by looking around in the world for issues.

How many of these instances show <u>place</u> referring directly to the world, like "orange" or "apple"? (Occasionally a text referent is too far away to appear in the line, but there is usually a clue – just guess.)

How would you answer Question C?

5. When can <u>place</u> be used dismissively, asks Question D, and for the answer to that we can consult the datafile **17_theplace.doc**. This concordance is a very small, unbiased selection of <u>place</u> used with only the definite article. It is not as tidily displayed as the others because some extra cotext has been included in several of the instances.

First of all, read through it carefully and note any instances where you feel the writer or speaker has a poor impression of the place in question, or refers to it casually. Find any clues in the cotext, and summarise your findings in an answer to Question D.

6. We now turn to the last question, concerning the use of <u>place</u> to mean where someone lives. The datafile for this part of the task is **17_tomyplace.doc**. This concordance was made by retrieving all the instances of <u>to my place</u> and selecting every sixth instance. This gave 25 instances, and two were removed; one was a song title <u>Come on Over to My Place</u>, and although appropriate it was one of a list and so the cotext was irrelevant; the other was an instance of <u>place</u> meaning one's position in a sports team.

First check that in these instances <u>place</u> means where the speaker or writer lives or works. Do you think that <u>my</u> is essential to this meaning? Do you think that <u>to</u> is essential? If these are optional what alternatives can you think of? You might get a clue from **17_place1.doc**.

7. Now look further to the left of <u>to</u> and note any repeated words and phrases in the concordance. Summarise these findings and the others in an answer to Question E.

8. Review your findings about <u>place</u>. Of the information you have gathered, consider

(a) how much you were already quite clearly aware of
(b) how much you recognise as correct although you might not have been able to recall it
(c) how much is new information that fits in with your idea about the word
(d) any unexpectedly new information.

Remember that this task has picked out just a few strands of the meaning and use of <u>place</u> in English. It has ignored the frequent use of the word in connection with position or ranking in competitions and lists, and many common phrases.

Datafile 17_place1.doc

1	we all need to feel we have a	place	in society. Most of us get that
2	Telfer believes that there is still a	place	for a little winding-up of the
3	I'll take you to a	place	I know. Beautiful stuff. Wear one
4	ring about it, that of a far-away	place	that nobody can spell, that nobody
5	these genes together in the first	place	, but if it is too common, the
6	city of Arles became the first	place	to experience power cuts. One
7	system for jumping quickly from one	place	to another on a moon rather than
8	An inquest may not be the perfect	place	to decide whether someone should be
9	his girlfriend Jessica Pagent's	place	is his second home. His is a close,
10	In a long analysis of France's	place	in Europe, he said the 'Franco-
11	believed the world would be a safer	place	if the Soviet Union too possessed
12	what hour the ceasefire should take	place	. 'They couldn't find for six hours
13	McKee. The show will take	place	at Belfast city centre's Boucher
14	we hope that if any crime has taken	place	that those responsible for it will
15	accommodation has obviously taken	place	. (9) Authority flows from such a
16	exhibitions and demonstrations taking	place	at over 20 venues around the City
17	football championships are taking	place	in Lagos, with twenty-one teams
18	is like a virus. It's all over the	place	. Rampant corruption. Everybody's
19	so, yes. The one your contact in the	Place	of Power mentioned might be coming
20	and palmists to the ghat, the	place	of cremation at the water's edge.
21	dotted unobtrusively about the	place	and reporting back to control." As
22	like to be fighting Hearts for third	place	in Scottish football but it is too
23	to pay thousands of dollars to	place	their ads on such prime locations
24	military two and the moneyed six took	place	in Kuwait last month, to no avail.
25	Sherman Antitrust Act in 1890 took	place	in an atmosphere of general public

Datafile 17_place2.doc

1	spot price. Alternatively, you can	place	an order for later delivery; in
2	recruiters of graduates continue to	place	emphasis on spring recruitment,
3	The report also calls for society to	place	less value on slimness. This
4	down at our end." Never again will I	place	a bet on a Group match. No wonder
5	both singles and doubles would	place	a heavy burden on one player, and
6	great power. Such limitations can	place	a strain on the strongest of
7	a foreign land. Of course he should	place	more trust in his captain,
8	the real estate market which would	place	further pressure on banks and would
9	lives. To value something means to	place	importance on it. Of course,
10	is expected to urge them to	place	restrictions on the sale of alcohol
11	In the old church people do not	place	their hearts and faith in God, but
12	in this case, the premium that women	place	on economic and material resources.
13	Japan, and the government managed to	place	the blame on Roosevelt, who had
14	votes, the administration agreed to	place	limits on mandatory spending

Datafile 17_place3.doc

1	A few years ago I stood at just such a	place	, panting and gasping in the thin air.
2	his household sailed to a landfall at a	place	called Blacksark, an ice mountain.
3	and he not only provided me with a	place	to stay, but kept me employed with
4	documentary on the building itself. In a	place	like this, you're never short of
5	For the region to remain an attractive	place	to live and work and for industrial
6	s that then? do you know the car	place	? Mm. Yeah. It's up
7	was a dingy, threatening and dangerous	place	. The merchandise mainly consisted of
8	right,' Julie said. 'This is a gathering	place	for the neighbourhood crowd. They come
9	Southampton has not been a good	place	for us in recent seasons and we know
10	Ramos was rejected. Very Ice	Place	to get married A FITNESS
11	It was not, she said, the 'ideal'	place	for a man who wished to hide his
12	their careers in Europe, NOT the one	place	that matters most . . . America. So why
13	on the meaning and value of that	place	. The selections that follow offer
14	regain its 1970s reputation as 'the	place	to be'. Now if BT could decide how to
15	and the sanctuary is built at the	place	where it is killed. Or a domestic
16	inch through the narrow passage. Not the	place	to suffer from claustrophobia, I
17	said, 'The cops will be all over this	place	in a few minutes. That should slow
18	only in Danzig. In other words, this	place	has even a kind of apocalyptic
19	of safety and plenty. We offer this	place	to you." Apparently it worked. Old-
20	in 1821 varied greatly from place to	place	; one lot of islanders who proved

Datafile 17_theplace.doc

1 'The **place** was run like a prison camp. From the moment we arrived, this little man made our life a misery.

2 Definitely the flat, but I am so rarely there . . . Every time I walk through the door, it is like seeing the **place** for the first time.

3 The people who run the **place** are pitching for local trade with the promise of Park Road ambience making its way northside.

4 on strict condition you do not mention the **place** for fear hordes of Australian tourists will descend, spoiling it.

5 I'd sold myself cheap and I knew it. Teddy was never really big on selling the **place**, you know. He just didn't want the responsibility.

6 players know he will show them no favours while he is sorting the **place** out. Success? It's not just this season that Aberdeen have been underachieving.

7 My God have you seen the **place**? . . . It's pretty grim isn't it.

8 A. my mum's sister kept saying you know Well you are going to move here like eventually erm so you might as well just leave.
B. Mm.
A. you know I mean like Julie here to get you know so they get used to the **place**
B. Mm.

9 I had seen one or two women about the **place**. It was an insupportable situation and Felicity was a fool to go on enduring it.

10 Neighbours Celebrate As Child Molester Is Butchered At Home; Revenge Mob Kill Perv. Local councillor John Wilson read them all with a sense of outrage. "I lived there for 23 years and I didn't recognise the **place**".

11 Everyone laughed at us when the motormouth manager, John Sitton, sacked the captain half-way through a match and challenged the whole team to a fight in front of the TV cameras. Barry Hearn bought the club, tidied up the **place** . . .

12 Well, the **place** seems pretty normal . . . Lots of dykes of all ages colours and descriptions, but so far no weirdos.

Datafile 17_tomyplace.doc

1	Sparky,' said Sillett. 'He came	to my place	and did some work on my house.
2	each way to get from my home	to my place	of business at Milton. If the
3	in the past when he'd commute	to my place	and just sit by my shoulder and
4	I'd feel better if we went	to my place	.' 'Colma?' She nodded. 'If
5	she said. You could go down	to my place	in the Cities." I'm staying. But
6	noticed. 'No, I'm going on back	to my place	. But could you maybe just tuck it
7	it felt natural. I walked back	to my place	and knelt down for the first time
8	asked if she could come back	to my place	. She got her overnight bag and we
9	What was I to do? I took her	to my place	and left her asleep in my spare
10	to invite him (and my friend)	to my place	for drinks." THE VERDICT: 'I liked
11	if it took two hours to get	to my place	. So we could go back and get
12	the television, then returned	to my place	beside Sylvie. She snuggled close
13	airplane. Jim brought him up	to my place	and said, you know, 'Here's my
14	rings and bring everything over	to my place	to cook. Come over when you've got
15	further. Then we go back	to my place	, make love and it's awful. He's a
16	for me, she would come	to my place	for the poems. Today, after I'd got
17	is begin to make my way back	to my place	. It's quite a walk from here. I'll
18	and followed me downstairs	to my place	. The first thing I did was make
19	I think so Come up	to my place	and let me show you my homunculi."
20	smoke is gone. 'Let's go	to my place	because I'll be happy,' he had
21	drink? Or shall we just go back	to my place	?" I should have been outraged, but
22	Why don't you come round	to my place	tomorrow and you can show me the
23	and Muslim girls), Fancy coming	to my place	, or fancy coming to see some of my

Task 17

Key

1. The commonest word is <u>take</u> and its inflections, to the left of <u>place</u>; there are eight instances.

2. <u>To take place</u> means to occur; it is a typical example of an IDIOM because the usual meanings of <u>take</u> and <u>place</u> are quite different, and the meaning "occur" cannot be worked out from them. Also the idiom does not allow another word in between <u>take</u> and <u>place</u>, and although <u>take</u> can be inflected, <u>place</u> is invariable, and there is no phrase <u>take places</u>.

Of the other meanings and uses of <u>place</u> in this concordance, only one occurs more than twice, in my analysis. In nos. 6, 8 and 11 <u>place</u> is modified – in no. 6 by the ordinal numeral <u>first</u>, and in the others by an adjective, <u>perfect</u> and <u>safer</u>. The structure is roughly:

PLACE-NAME BE ARTICLE ADJECTIVE <u>place</u> . . .

Other repeated meanings are:

- a social or political position relative to others: nos. 1 and 10
- a location which is deliberately kept vague: nos. 2 and 3
- a title or a definition in the phrase <u>a place of . . .</u> : nos. 19 and 20.

Answer to Question A

Our conclusion has to be, on the basis of this evidence, that the commonest meaning of <u>place</u> is in the idiom <u>take place</u>, which means roughly "occur". In the largest collections of English the idiom accounts for more than one in every six occurrences of the word <u>place</u>, and since this word combines in many different ways to make a lot of meanings, it is unlikely that any of the other meanings is more frequent than this one.

If you did not guess this, it is not surprising; our intuitions are trained to see meanings as attached to single words, as in a dictionary (where you will find this meaning only as a minor usage under <u>take</u> or <u>place</u>). So when we are thinking about the meaning of <u>place</u> we do not automatically think of combinations of words.

3. Rephrasing of the lines in **17_place2.doc**:

1. . . . you can order for later delivery
2. . . . continue to emphasise spring recruitment
3. . . . to value slimness less

4. Never again will I bet on a Group match
5. ... would burden one player heavily ...
6. ... can strain the strongest ...
7. ... he should trust his captain more
8. ... which would pressure banks further ...
9. [not possible]
10. ... urge them to restrict the sale of alcohol ...
11. [not possible]
12. [not possible]
13. ... managed to blame Roosevelt ...
14. ... agreed to limit mandatory spending ...

No.	Noun object	Change	Notes
1	order	order (verb)	noun and verb are identical
2	emphasis	emphasise	cognate verb
3	value	value (verb)	noun and verb are identical
4	bet	bet (verb)	noun and verb are identical
5	burden	burden (verb)	noun and verb are identical
		heavy → heavily	adjective → adverb
6	strain	strain (verb)	noun and verb are identical
7	trust	trust more	noun and verb are identical
			adjective and adverb are identical
8	pressure	pressure (verb)	noun and verb are identical
		further	adjective and adverb are identical
9	importance	[none]	no cognate verb in modern English
10	restrictions	restrict	cognate verb
11	hearts and faith	[none]	no cognate verb
12	premium	[none]	no cognate verb
13	blame	blame (verb)	noun and verb are identical
14	limits	limit (verb)	noun and verb are identical

Conclusion

A large number of words in English can be used as either nouns or verbs, and in their uninflected forms are identical. In these cases the structure:

place ARTICLE NOUN PREPOSITION ...

can be rephrased as:

VERB PREPOSITION ...

and place disappears from the sentence. In other cases the noun and verb may not be identical but are COGNATE, in that they are obviously related historically to each other. The meaning changes very little, though several of the sentences sound much more natural with the verb–object structure. In no. 9, the English verb "import" used to mean "have importance", but it would not have fitted this cotext.

This almost accidental feature of English thus allows the verb place to be removed without a lot of damage to the creation of meaning. It is not the only example, because place is often used in a kind of support role. You may have noticed that in **17_place1.doc** the instances of the structure:

ADJ place

could be rephrased without place:

(?) An inquest may not be perfect to decide . . .
the world would be safer if . . .

I have queried the first instance because the following infinitive is almost ungrammatical in this combination – ". . . perfect for deciding . . ." sounds much more natural.

Answer to Question B

Where the word place has a support role it can often be omitted in a rephrasing, though the result may not always sound natural. English seems to prefer transitive clauses to intransitive ones, and place is often used to "carry" a noun object, even when the same word could stand as an intransitive verb. English also seems to prefer adjectives to be attached to nouns, and place is one of the common nouns that are used just to "carry" an adjective.

4.

No.	Text referent	Mechanism	Notes
1	[in wider cotext]	such a	backward reference continues; see comment
2	Blacksark	a . . . called	naming
3		a . . . to stay	infinitive phrase identifies the kind of place
4	the building itself	a . . . like this	this is direct reference to location of utterance
5	the region	an . . . to live	place carries adjective attractive
6		the car	shared knowledge of a location
7	[supermarket]	a . . .	place carries adjectives dingy, etc.
8		This	This is direct reference to location of utterance
9	Southampton	a . . . for us . . .	place carries adjective good, etc.
10	[the South Pole]	. . . to . . .	heading of a news story
11	[a funeral]	It	backward reference continues
12	America	the one . . .	forward reference
13	place	that	curious instance of writing about "place"
14	[embassy]	its . . . the . . . to	see comment

No.	Text referent	Mechanism	Notes
15		the . . . where	where clause identifies the location
16	[passage]	the	infinitive phrase identifies the kind of place
17		this	this is direct reference to location of utterance
18	Danzig . . .	this	this is direct reference to location of utterance
19		this	direct reference to location – see comment
20		from . . . to . . .	phrase from place to place gives vague location

Cases for comment

- No. 1. The referent is a long way back in the cotext; it refers to a point of decision in mountain climbing.
- No. 14. There is a familiar phrase "the X to Y", which we interpret as "the X you should Y" – corpus examples include, among hundreds, the place to visit, the movie to see this week, the album to go for.
- No. 19. The previous cotext is:

  Picture, for instance, the potting shed and say temptingly, "We ask you to move to a place of safety and plenty. . . ."

  It could be argued that the reference of place in no. 19 is a backward reference to the potting shed, but the likelihood is that the utterance is made in a location in or near the potting shed, and so the instance is best interpreted as a direct reference to a location in the outside world.

Answer to Question C

If the instances we have examined are typical of the way English is used – and we have no reason to suspect that they are not – then we conclude that place is not used to refer directly to a location in the world. Let us review the evidence in the table above; there are five instances in which direct reference is made to a location, and in all cases it is the immediate location of the utterance. The referring word is this, not place. In the other fifteen instances – 75% – the referent of place is to be found in the text, before or after, or there is no clear referent at all, as in nos. 6 and 20.

It is clear from these instances that place is one of the many important nouns in English which are rarely used alone. (For an account of them, see Sinclair et al., 1990, page 19.) By "used alone" is meant occurring as the entire subject or object of a structure, with an article only if the noun is countable and singular. There are no such instances of place in our concordance, and they are only likely to occur when a wider cotext makes them possible. So in the following instance a place occurs on its own but clearly refers to apartments:

> People mainly live in apartments, which are all very stylish and beautifully equipped with German gadgets. Half the population rent a place and half own one.

In any case these are uncommon events. Nevertheless it is clear that many accomplished users of English are not aware that place rarely refers to a location; a textbook for teaching English contains the instruction:

> Think of three places near your school.

There is no such thing as "a place" in this usage without further specification of what kind of place is meant; the sentence as it stands is ungrammatical.

To summarise, the simple answer to Question C is "No, not without support for the meaning, because places have to be identified in texts and not in the world."

5.

No.	Evidence/clue	Pejorative/dismissive/casual
1	prison camp . . . misery	pejorative
2		dismissive reference to the place where he lives
3	pitching for	uncomplimentary reference to new shop
4	hordes . . . spoiling	prediction about decline
5	cheap	distancing – neither party interested
6	no favours . . . sorting . . . out . . . underachieving	pejorative
7	My God . . . pretty grim	pejorative
8	get used to	casual, in very informal conversation
9	insupportable . . . fool	dismissive – not a good place to be
10	. . . Mob Kill Perv . . . , etc.	dismissive and distancing
11	tidied up, etc.	pejorative
12	dykes . . . weirdos	pejorative – normal is ironic

Although the range of meaning is quite considerable, all the instances show a negative SEMANTIC PROSODY. It can be merely a matter of distancing a location from the speaker/writer, or casual as in no. 8, but it is always on the negative side. There are occasional instances – not in the selection above – where it refers affectionately to a location; fewer than 1% of instances show place collocating with love, but there is often another element of meaning around that suggests insincerity or some major qualification. Instances include:

he quickly fell in love with the **place** with its leafy lanes and smart houses. . . . But it was a while before he discovered the flip side of the peaceful village.

I fell in love with the **place** despite its position.

I always said I'd never move back to London but I love the **place**, I really do.

The words <u>But</u>, <u>despite</u> and <u>really</u> show the qualifications.

The answer to Question D is that when <u>the place</u> is used without any other modifier or qualifier, it is nearly always at least a little dismissive, and often quite a lot.

6. In all the instances, <u>place</u> means where the speaker or writer lives. Although <u>my</u> is likely to be very frequent here, any of the possessive adjectives (except <u>its</u>) will provide the necessary COLLIGATION. Also you may have noticed in no. 9 of **17_place1.doc** the following:

his girlfriend Jessica Pagent's place is his second home.

This instance suggests that a noun group naming a person, with the possessive marker '<u>s</u> attached to it, can also fulfil the requirements of colligation. This is confirmed in the corpus in instances such as:

We ended up going to Mum and Dad's place.

Turning to the preposition <u>to</u>, it is easy to show that several other prepositions can occur there without disturbing the meaning of <u>place</u>. <u>At</u>, <u>from</u> and <u>in</u> are quite frequent, though <u>to</u> is the commonest. The instance quoted above from **17_place1.doc** contributes to this query also, because in that instance <u>place</u> is the head of the noun group which is subject of the clause, and so there will be no preposition. This is not common, but quite a normal structure.

We can conclude from this that the CORE of the phrase meaning where someone lives is:

possessive <u>place</u>

and that another typical colligation is with a preposition, notably <u>to</u>.

7. The adverbs <u>back</u> (6) and <u>up</u> (2) recur, and from a larger selection I can add <u>over</u>, <u>down</u>, <u>home</u> and <u>round</u>, which are single occurrences in this small concordance but quite frequent as collocates of <u>to my place</u>. So almost half of the instances have this additional adverb. Also repeated are forms of the verb "come", which we can add to the verbs found at the next place to the left. The prominent verbs are forms of "come" and "go"; of the others, <u>get</u>, <u>commute</u>, <u>walked</u>, <u>took her</u>, <u>returned</u>, <u>brought (him)</u>, <u>bring (everything)</u>, <u>make my way</u>

and <u>followed (me)</u> are all semantically close to the two principal collocates, and <u>invite</u> refers to another aspect of someone's home.

With this evidence we can postulate the existence of a LEXICAL ITEM as follows:

(a) The CORE consists of a possessive adjective, principally <u>my</u>, followed by the word form <u>place</u>.

(b) As well as this COLLIGATION within the core, there is another colligation with a preposition, of which the COLLOCATE <u>to</u> is the typical realisation. The preposition comes just in front of the core.

(c) There is also an optional colligation with certain adverbs, COLLOCATES <u>back</u>, <u>round</u>, <u>over</u> and <u>home</u>, positioned just in front of the preposition. This sub-class of adverb overlaps significantly with locational prepositions.

(d) There is a semantic PREFERENCE for movement, often realised by one of the two commonest verbs of movement, "come" and "go", taking a position to the left of the colligations.

(e) The overall semantic PROSODY of this item is to give a little of the informal warmth of someone's home, used mainly in invitations, and different from "home" in that it is less permanent and may physically be just the apartment that a person is staying in for a time. The essence is the personal nature of the invitation.

8. The response to this item has to be personal, because it depends on your knowledge of English and of linguistics, and the kind of interest you take in languages generally. I give my own response below, but since I have worked on this word for some time my recollection may not be typical.

The knowledge that <u>take place</u> is the commonest use of <u>place</u> is category (b); I would not have retrieved this or guessed it, but when I see the evidence it is no surprise; however, I have been noticing for many years that the most frequent use of a word is in a phrasal combination, so I am almost expecting it. Dictionaries are clearly not expecting it; it usually occurs towards the end of an entry.

The use of <u>place</u> in phrases such as <u>place an order</u> is category (c). I was aware that <u>place</u> is a very common verb, and as such it can almost be predicted to have a support role; but the systematic relationship between the verb–object construction and the intransitive verb, where the object and the intransitive verb are the same word or cognates, is an interesting feature of English, and I had not noted it in relation to <u>place</u>.

The information that <u>place</u> is not used to refer directly to locations in the world was completely new to me, and I think it will be new for most lexicographers, grammarians and language teachers, because I cannot find any mention of it in reference works. Most dictionaries consider this "meaning" as the main one, although the corpus evidence is that it does not exist. This information is category (d).

The dismissive quality of <u>the place</u> is partly category (a) and part (b). Because of phrases like "all over the place" I was not surprised to meet this meaning, but I could not have recalled the detail; the apparent counterexamples like <u>I fell in love with the place</u> are still to be explored.

I already knew that <u>place</u> could mean <u>home</u> (category (a)) and I could have exemplified this with a sentence like "Come round to my place", without knowing which words were necessary and which just helped the atmosphere. So the whole lexical item, and its role as an invitation, are in category (b) – available to me, but not consciously.

Task 18

Singular and plural

We are taught to think of grammatical choices like singular versus plural, active versus passive, as delivering a piece of information that makes only minor and consequential changes to the meaning of the words in their cotexts. So we can expect the singular of a countable noun like "clock" to occur with the article "a", whereas the plural "clocks" will not occur with "a" except in a few well-known cases like "a few clocks".

Otherwise the patterns of usage of the two words are expected to be rather similar. So we assume that there is in the vocabulary of English an item that we call the noun "clock", which has two forms "clock" and "clocks" (and maybe "clock's" and "clocks'" as well). The only difference in meaning between the forms is that of grammatical number – that is implicit in the idea of recognising two forms of the same word. In computational linguistics there is a similar distinction made between an individual FORM and a LEMMA; in lexicography a similar distinction is made between word-form and HEADWORD.

Let us examine this assumption a little more closely, particularly the assumption that the meaning does not radically change when the form does.

1. The datafile **18_clock_colls.doc** contains fifty of the most important collocates of the word form "clock", selected from a large corpus by a statistical test called T-SCORE. The datafile **18_clocks_colls.doc** has the same information for the plural "clocks". Compare the two and note which collocates they share. Does this overlap support the idea that the two forms have the same range of meanings?

2. Look at the remainder of the **18_clock_colls.doc** file. Are these words also likely to appear with clocks, or do you think they particularly go with clock? Do the same for **18_clock_colls.doc** with respect to clock.

3. Now repeat steps 1 and 2 using the collocation files for eye (**18_eye_colls.doc**) and eyes (**18_eyes_colls.doc**).

4. Study the collocation file for eye a little more; can you suggest some idiomatic phrases that would account for otherwise unusual collocations?

5. Can you think of an explanation of the relationship between eye and eyes from a collocational perspective?

Datafile 18_clock_colls.doc

o	eight	night	twelve	against
at	five	ticking	11	wall
morning	news	clock	minutes	10
the	back	afternoon	till	hour
nine	seven	about	tower	up
six	on	turn	after	when
round	three	time	before	00
around	alarm	evening	biological	grandfather
ten	eleven	until	working	shortly
four	two	one	miles	watch

Datafile 18_clocks_colls.doc

and	timepieces	grandfather	put	tick
watches	our	other	go	jewellery
time	clocks	all	wall	glass
alarm	forward	set	clock	inner
biological	accurate	midnight	silver	strike
body	reset	ticking	these	lamps
atomic	cuckoo	antique	were	when
back	furniture	up	stop	exports
their	hour	including	through	barometers
are	internal	your	circadian	mirrors

Datafile 18_eye_colls.doc: the most frequent collocates of <u>eye</u>

a	an	bird	black	blind
blink	cast	catch	catching	caught
close	contact	corner	eagle	eye
for	her	his	keep	keeping
kept left	level	look	meets	midnight
mind	my	naked	on	one
opener	private	public	right	s
see	shadow	sharp	the	turn
turned	twinkle	under	view	watchful
with	witness	witnesses	your	

Datafile 18_eyes_colls.doc: the most frequent collocates of <u>eyes</u>

and	before	black	blue	bright
brown	close	closed	dark	ears
eyes	face	fixed	green	grey
hair	he	head	her	him
his	into	light	lips	look
looked	me	met mouth	my	nose
open	opened	our	pale	rolled
s	saw	see	she	shut
skin	staring	tears	their	through
were	wide	with your		

Task 18

Key

1. There are nine words that appear in both collocation files:

alarm back biological grandfather hour ticking time wall watch(es)

Central to the notion of a clock is <u>time</u>, and the main divisions of a clock are the <u>hours</u>. An <u>alarm</u> clock is one of the commonest types, and in earlier times the <u>grandfather</u> clock was popular. Older clocks could be heard <u>ticking</u>, and this is so closely associated with clocks that many of the modern electronic ones have ticks although they do not need them. Many modern clocks hang on a <u>wall</u>. When clocks go fast, or when we change to a winter time, we turn the clocks <u>back</u>. The idea of a <u>biological</u> clock is fairly new but widely used. A small version of a clock is called a <u>watch</u>, but we must not jump to conclusions here since <u>watch</u> is also a common verb for observing something, and quite often clocks are what are watched.

All these collocates provide evidence to confirm that the meaning of <u>clock</u> and <u>clocks</u> is very similar.

2. <u>O'clock</u> is the most significant collocation in the concordance of <u>clock</u>, occurring in more than half the lines, and many of the collocations of <u>clock</u> (but not <u>clocks</u>) are connected with <u>o'clock</u>; in fact its cotext shows that it is best seen as part of a different lexical item from <u>clock</u>. The written forms of all the numbers from <u>one</u> to <u>twelve</u>, and the figures <u>10</u> and <u>11</u> are all prominent, and words to do with periods of the day, <u>afternoon</u>, <u>evening</u>, <u>morning</u> and <u>night</u>, are also attracted by <u>o'clock</u>, and, in relation to radio broadcasts, <u>news</u>. None of these words are in the top fifty collocates of <u>clock</u> without <u>o'</u>.

Among the collocations of <u>clocks</u> there are some other plural nouns – <u>barometers</u>, <u>lamps</u>, <u>mirrors</u>, <u>timepieces</u>, <u>watches</u> – and some mass nouns whose meaning is a grouping of individual items – <u>collection</u>, <u>furniture</u>, <u>glass</u>, <u>jewellery</u>. There is also a small set of words that recall the practice in many societies of putting clocks back an hour in the autumn and forward an hour in the spring: <u>back</u>, <u>forward</u>, <u>reset</u>, <u>set</u>, <u>midnight</u>.

There is thus little evidence that the singular and plural of the lemma "clock" have different meanings; most of their differences in collocation can be ascribed to the difference between singular and plural, and the separate lexical item whose CORE is <u>o'clock</u>.

3. Collocational analysis of <u>eye</u> and <u>eyes</u>.

A. There are nine word forms that appear in both files:

black close her his look my s see with

Related forms occur also: <u>eyes</u> has <u>closed</u>, <u>he</u>, <u>him</u>, <u>looked</u>, <u>me</u>, <u>open</u>, <u>opened</u> and <u>saw</u>; while <u>eye</u> has <u>opener</u>, making the compound noun <u>eye-opener</u>.

<u>Eye</u> collocates with itself – that is to say, it occurs twice in a short space of text. <u>Eyes</u> does the same, but the two forms do not collocate with each other. Compare <u>clocks</u>, which collocates with both <u>clocks</u> and <u>clock</u>.

The other shared words – the preposition <u>with</u> and possessives <u>her</u>, <u>his</u>, <u>my</u> and <u>'s</u> – are so common that they are unlikely to distinguish meanings unless there is a very clear separation, which does not appear to be the case here. The verbs "look" and "see" express what most people would take to be part of the CORE meaning of <u>eye</u>, and <u>close</u> and "open" refer to the fact that the eyes can be covered by the eyelids.

The remaining shared word, <u>black</u>, is interesting because although it collocates with both forms it has a very different lexical function; <u>a black eye</u> is an eye injured by a blow or an accident, and may not always be coloured black, while <u>black eyes</u> are more commonly eyes which are naturally coloured black. Here <u>black eye</u> is a component of an idiomatic phrase, and <u>black eyes</u> is just a reasonably common collocation.

B. We will examine first the collocations of <u>eyes</u>, ignoring the pronouns and possessives. These can be roughly classified as "colours", "body parts" and "relevant verbs"; those shared with <u>eyes</u> are bracketed.

<u>colours, hues, etc.</u>
(black), blue, brown, green, grey; bright, dark, pale; wide

<u>body parts</u>
ears, face, hair, head, lips, mouth, nose, tears

<u>relevant verbs</u>
(close, closed, open, opened, see, saw), shut, staring

The colours are all the normal eye colours, and the hues are also familiar collocates, and <u>wide</u> relates to the degree of opening of the eyes.

The body parts are those in the vicinity of the eyes, except <u>tears</u> which appear *in* the eyes.

The verbs express the facts that eyes can be covered by eyelids, moved in different directions, and focus on one place for a long time. The expression of the basic function of sight is shared with <u>eye</u>.

In summary, the collocates of <u>eyes</u> are confirmed by the intuition as familiar and relating to the meaning of the eye as the organ of sight.

C. The picture with <u>eye</u> is rather different; perhaps the first thing to note is the absence of collocates like those we have just seen occurring with <u>eyes</u>. Words such as <u>bird</u>, <u>cast</u>, <u>contact</u>, <u>corner</u>, <u>eagle</u>, <u>keep</u>, <u>meet</u>, <u>mind</u>, <u>naked</u>, <u>private</u>, <u>public</u> and <u>witness</u> have little to do with sight. (There is a rather rare word "cast" for a disease of the eyes, which has no effect on the patterns recorded here.) Certainly there are some words of sight and seeing, like <u>blink</u>, <u>twinkle</u> and <u>watchful</u>, but most of these are specific types of seeing; only <u>look</u> is general.

4. The absence of ordinary and expected collocates like colours and body parts gives rise to a suspicion that the singular form is not typically used to refer to the organ of sight. But if the collocates are combined, like <u>bird</u> and <u>view</u>, or <u>turn</u> and <u>blind</u>, we see the skeletons of some fairly fixed idiomatic phrases – here are the main ones that include words from the collocation list:

- a bird's eye view
- turn a blind eye
- in the blink of an eye (and some NEG <u>blink an eye</u>)
- cast an eye over (variants: an adjective – <u>cold</u>, <u>critical</u>, . . . ; <u>on</u> instead of <u>over</u>)
- catch my eye (variants: any possessive adjective, and <u>the eye of . . .</u> phrases; POSS <u>eye <was> caught</u>)
- eye contact
- out of the corner of his eye (variants: <u>from</u> and any possessive adjective)
- eagle-eye or eagle-eyed
- with an eye for (variants: <u>has</u> or <u>got</u> instead of <u>with</u>, an adjective modifying <u>eye</u>)
- keep an eye on; keep an eye out for
- at eye level
- look him in the eye (variants: <u>him</u> can be any person or animal)
- a look in her eye (any possessive adjective)
- meets his eye (variant: <u>his</u> can be any possessive adjective)
- the mind's eye (variant: <u>the</u> can be any possessive)
- with the naked eye (variant: <u>to</u>)
- private eye
- in the public eye
- eye-shadow
- a sharp eye
- a twinkle in his eye (variant: any possessive adjective)
- under the watchful eye of . . .
- eye witness (witnesses)

If we ignore Midnight Eye because it is the name of a US musical ensemble, we have shown at least the principal patterning of the collocates of <u>eye</u>. They are largely unlike those of <u>eyes</u> because their meaning is much more complex than a reference to an organ of sight; they concern monitoring, critical examination and various points of view. Where <u>eye</u> refers to an organ of sight it is often modified by <u>left</u> or <u>right</u> and deals with injury or disease.

5. Once the above facts are established by the collocations, it is clear that there is a lot more difference in meaning between <u>eye</u> and <u>eyes</u> than just singular

and plural. It is easy enough to understand why this might have happened; since eyes normally occur in pairs then the singular form will not be much used, and so it is available for combining into figurative phrases like those above.

To a competent user of English, this fact is immediately confirmed by what we call intuition; whereas "blue eyes" is normal, there is something odd about "blue eye". In a narrative or conversation no-one will misinterpret "I caught his eye" as implying that he threw one of his eyes at me; "I caught his eyes" will not occur, although in the physical situation both of his eyes are likely to be involved.

However, we seem to be able to use intuition to confirm corpus evidence, but not always to predict it accurately. When we think of the pairs "clock, clocks" and "eye, eyes" we do not think of them as having a different semantic relationship, but when the corpus evidence shows how different they are we can immediately confirm this. The corpus has helped us to bring out latent knowledge about the language.

Glossary of terms in corpus linguistics used in this book

ATTRIBUTIVE ADJECTIVE
An adjective that comes in front of a noun which it modifies – contrast with PREDICATIVE. [Task 12]

COGNATE
Where words from two word classes are clearly related to each other they are called cognates; so the adjective nice and the adverb nicely are cognates, and the verb decide and the noun decision are cognates, the second one being formed from the first. Sometimes cognates are identical, as in the many words in English which in their uninflected forms are either nouns or verbs – run, shout, drive, etc. [Task 17]

COLLIGATION
Colligation is similar to COLLOCATION in that they both concern the co-occurrence of linguistic features in a text. Colligation is the occurrence of a grammatical class or structural pattern with another one, or with a word or phrase. "Negative", "possessive" and "modal" are the kinds of largely grammatical categories that figure in colligation. The term was first used by J. R. Firth, and has been widened a little for corpus work. [Tasks 10, 16 and 17]

COLLOCATION
This is a general term for two or more words occurring near each other in a text. It is used in several rather different ways by different writers on lexis; some reserve it for collocations which are statistically significant, and use the term CO-OCCURRENCE for the simple physical event; others require that a collocation must map precisely onto a complete grammatical structure, like a noun phrase. [Task 13]

CONCORDANCE
A concordance is an index to the places in a text where particular words and phrases occur. In modern corpus linguistics, the normal format of presentation is KWIC.

CO-OCCURRENCE
Any two or more words occurring in a text within a small SPAN is a co-occurrence. This is the most basic term for lexical patterning – see also COLLIGATION, COLLOCATION, CO-SELECTION.

CORE
The CORE is one of the obligatory elements of the structure of a lexical item, and it consists of one or more words which are either invariable or subject to

certain grammatical variations. Variation beyond the limits makes it impossible for the lexical item to create its meaning or even to be recognised. The permitted variation – in some cases only – is (a) grammatical inflection, and (b) membership of a specified grammatical class or a lexicalisation of this class.

"CORE MEANING"

This term is taken from general discussions about vocabulary, and is quite different from the CORE of a lexical item. The CORE MEANING of a word is said to be an intuitive notion about what is its main literal meaning. So, for example, "eye" means the part of the body in the face that is used for vision, and the eye of a storm, the centre of it, is considered a FIGURATIVE extension of the meaning. People sometimes also consider the core meaning to be the earliest recorded meaning in the historical development of the word, and expect that it will be the commonest meaning in texts. Neither of these impressions is consistently supported by evidence.

CO-SELECTION

In English orthography, the letter q must be followed by u. All the other letters, including u, are by comparison much less restricted; certainly there are many combinations that do not occur or that occur very rarely, but there are so many combinations that do occur that the overall impression is that of freedom.

The basic notion of a word is that it is a "free form" – it can occur without any requirements on the cotext. No other word is required in its vicinity. Nevertheless we note many exceptions to this notion – for example, the verb dote has to name the object of the doting. In most cases this is done by using a prepositional phrase with on, occasionally over.

The letters q and u are a co-selection, and so is dote on, despite the slight variability of the latter. CO-SELECTION is a type of COLLOCATION.

Students of a language, and many users, are aware of the relatively fixed co-selections like dote on; but there can be a lot of variation among co-selected words, as the verb incur demonstrates [Tasks 8 and 14].

COTEXT

The COTEXT of a word or phrase is the group of words that occur on either side of it in a text. It can also be called the "verbal context" or the "verbal environment". The number of words in the cotext is not fixed, because individual words vary in the influence they exert on the cotext, the range and direction of their influence. For practical purposes a fairly arbitrary figure is set of four or five words on either side; experience shows that this size of cotext (called the SPAN) is sufficient for most descriptive purposes, and not so large that a great deal of extraneous material is also collected. [Task 15]

FIGURATIVE

The FIGURATIVE meaning of a word is one which concerns abstract ideas rather than concrete physical ones, and it is used in contrast to the LITERAL meaning, from which it is often considered to be derived by "extension". So the literal meaning of "summit" is the top of a hill, but in modern journalism it more often means a meeting of important people. Metaphors of height are used in organisations to express importance, and the facts that climbing a mountain is difficult, and few people do it, add to the figurative meaning.

Idiomatic phrases usually have a FIGURATIVE meaning, and that has another feature to it, often considered as the defining feature of an IDIOM. The phrase is interpreted as a single unit whose meaning may seem unrelated, or only loosely related, to the words that make it up. So the phrase "turn a blind eye to" something means to ignore it. Once the meaning is known (but not before) the words can often be related to aspects of the meaning, and this process is sometimes used as an explanation of the relation between the literal and figurative types of meaning. But the example given arises out of a known historical event during the Battle of Trafalgar, where Admiral Lord Nelson, who had lost an eye in previous warfare, put his telescope to his blind eye and claimed he did not see a signal from his superior to withdraw. This is not retrievable from the words that make up the phrase.

FOCUSING

This is a type of CO-SELECTION between an adjective and a noun, where the adjective does not narrow the referential range of the noun (as "red" in "red pencils" does) but combines with the noun so that they make a meaning together. At times the adjective will draw attention to an aspect of the meaning of the noun, and at times it will indicate which of several possible meanings of the noun are relevant in the cotext; in some cases a noun meaning is hardly possible without the adjective, and in others the adjective acts like a catalyst in chemical reactions, providing a supportive environment for a particular noun meaning to be indicated. See SELECTIVE. [Task 5]

FORM

(also called "WORD FORM"). A sequence of characters chosen from letters of the alphabet, the apostrophe and the hyphen, that occur between spaces and other punctuation marks. Forms are the physical realisations of WORDS. This is the simplest item for the computer to search on, and still the commonest starting point for corpus investigation. See also LEMMA and HEADWORD.

HEADWORD

There are two quite different uses of this term, showing how rarely lexico-graphers and grammarians get together.

(a) In a dictionary, the headwords are the words that begin entries; they are usually printed a little bigger than the other words, and often stick out into the margin to make the entry easy to find. By convention, the headword is the uninflected form, so that the headword "steal" stands for the forms "steal", "steals", "stealing", "stole" and "stolen". See LEMMA for a very similar notion.

(b) In a grammar, a headword is the main word in a noun group or phrase; usually a noun, that comes after the articles, adjectives, etc., but before qualifying clauses and phrases. So in "a savings account for all children", "account" is the headword.

IDIOM

Everyone knows, in a way, what IDIOMS are, but it is very difficult to define them. There is something quite specific and local about their meaning. The most popular definition of an idiom is that it is a phrase that has a meaning that cannot be predicted from the individual meanings of the words that make it up. Idioms that are often quoted to illustrate this unique kind of meaning are, for example, kick the bucket, red herring and it's raining cats and dogs. These mean, respectively, to die, an irrelevant diversion, and it's raining very heavily. Although some of the words keep their normal meaning, e.g. raining, it is not possible to guess the meaning of the phrase as a whole.

This kind of definition is wholly inadequate, since after studying corpora we have no reason to believe that a word has "a" meaning that it keeps for itself, or even several meanings from which one is chosen in a cotext. The kind of idioms instanced above are merely fairly prominent examples of the need for a number of words to occur together to establish a meaning.

Many idioms show restrictions on the normal choices of word order and inflection – see Task 17, especially Key §2.

KWIC

"Key Word In Context" is the name of the best known organisation of a computer-generated CONCORDANCE, and it has been around for over forty years. The concordances in this book follow KWIC layout, in that the NODE word is placed in the centre of the citation and the whole set of citations is aligned by the first letter of the node word.

LEMMA, LEMMATISED

LEMMA is the term in computational linguistics for a collection of word forms, normally *inflections*, which vary in form according to morphological rules without (it is assumed) the meaning undergoing radical change. In lexicography the lemma is called the HEADWORD, and in common usage, if we refer to a "word" we usually mean the lemma and not the form.

In this book the distinction is carefully maintained, with word forms underlined and lemmas within quote marks. Task 18 examines the relationship between form and lemma.

LEXICALISED

Meaningful choices can be made in different ways; when a grammar is separated from the rest of language patterning, we see a network of choices, usually fairly simple and discrete, like number (singular and plural) and voice (active and passive). But very much the same choices can be made without the grammatical apparatus, using the meanings of ordinary words. So "He cannot come."

and "He is unable to come." are very close in meaning; the first uses the choice of negative (as against positive) and the modal <u>can</u>, while the second uses a word that contains a negative prefix and the meaning of ability; "He is prevented from coming." is quite similar again.

When choices of ordinary words are found making the same meanings as grammatical choices, we call those choices *lexicalised*. Linguistic descriptions will not be complete unless the grammatical and lexical choices are related to each other. [Task 11]

LITERAL

The literal meaning of a phrase is the one where each word is understood in its most characteristic sense, and there is no extra meaning that comes from putting the words next to each other. Literal meaning is often contrasted with FIGURATIVE meaning, where the phrase is interpreted as a single unit whose meaning may seem unrelated, or only loosely related, to the words that make it up. See also METAPHORICAL. [Tasks 4, 12, 15]

METAPHORICAL

A metaphor is a word or phrase which is interpreted not in a direct or LITERAL way, but with reference to a comparison. So if I say I have a mountain of paperwork to get through, I am not suggesting that the paper is thousands of metres high and so solid that it can be climbed, but that to me sitting at my desk it feels like a climber feels at the bottom of a mountain – that there is a lot of strenuous work ahead. In this example we say that "mountain" is used metaphorically. Metaphorical meaning is similar to FIGURATIVE meaning, but a little more specific. [Task 12]

NODE

In a KWIC concordance, the instances are aligned centrally around the word that has been the subject of the query; this word is called the NODE word; it is purely a device for helping the researcher and has no linguistic significance. Collocation is between two or more collocates, and it is arbitrary which the researcher selects as node in any particular investigation.

If the query concerns a phrase, one word in the phrase is chosen as the node. See SPAN for the way positions are calculated. [Task 2]

PREDICATIVE ADJECTIVE

One which occurs as complement to a verb, and does not modify a noun. Contrast with ATTRIBUTIVE.

PROSPECTION

Sometimes as we are reading or listening to language we encounter words and phrases that give us an idea of what lies ahead. The form of a question, for example, tells us that an answer is solicited, but not only that – it tells us that whatever is said next will be interpreted as some sort of reaction to the question. All possible responses are thus pre-classified, and the mechanism by which language does this is called PROSPECTION.

There is a lexical aspect to prospection also. Sometimes a phrasing sets up an expectation about what we are going to be told next. For example, if you read or hear that a country is "on the brink of" something, the words that will come into mind to complete the phrase will almost certainly refer to unpleasant things like war or recession.

REVERSAL

Sometimes the particular choice of words close to each other in a text produces a meaning that is not found in the individual meanings of the words chosen. When this happens regularly to the same phrase, it is called an IDIOM, but it often happens that a phrasing temporarily creates a meaning from the text that is not inherent in the normal usage of the individual words. These are unique meanings that will never be recorded in reference books. Corpus study suggests that reversal – when the text makes the meaning – is a much more frequent event than is commonly supposed. See Task 6 Key §5, and Task 12.

SELECTIVE

In contrast to FOCUSING, this is the familiar relationship between an adjective and the noun it modifies. In a referential view of meaning, the noun designates a set of objects or events and the adjective designates a subset – so "water", "cold water", "hot water". [Task 5]

SEMANTIC PREFERENCE

Sometimes in the structure of a phrase there is a clear preference for words of a particular meaning. The word class is not important, and any word with the appropriate meaning will do (though there are often collocational patterns within semantic preference). While the majority of the choices will show the preference clearly, there may be a small number of marginal cases where the preferred meaning has to be interpreted in a rather elastic fashion, and some which appear to be exceptions. For this reason we do not use a word like "restriction" instead of "preference". See Tasks 9 and 16.

SEMANTIC PROSODY

A corpus enables us to see words grouping together to make special meanings that relate not so much to their dictionary meanings as to the reasons why they were chosen together. This kind of meaning is called SEMANTIC PROSODY; it has been recognised in part as connotation, pragmatic meaning and attitudinal meaning, but it rarely appears in reference works that do not derive their evidence from corpora. The notion of prosody is taken from phonology; a prosody is a meaningful event that is not necessarily located in a particular unit of expression, but may spread over several.

The recognition that semantic prosody is a constant feature of text is one of the most important contributions of corpus work so far. Tasks 3, 14 and 16 show some of its operation, but it is present in most of the sections because it is central to the creation of meaning.

SIMILE

A figure of speech that expresses the resemblance of one thing to another of a different category, usually introduced by <u>as</u> or <u>like</u>. (*Collins English Dictionary*, 1998)

SINGLETON

A word form that occurs once only in a set that is derived from a concordance. The general name for such words in running text is *hapax legomena*.

SPAN

The distance between two collocating words, measured in words, is called the SPAN. If there are more than two the distance from the first to the last is the span. In the KWIC concordances that are presented in this book, the span is measured from the NODE to the COLLOCATE.

Positions in a span may be identified by calling the node "N", and using "+" and "−" for right and left; so the formula N+3 refers to the position three words to the right of the node word. If the node consists of more than one word, then N+1 is the first word to the right of the last word of the node.

T-SCORE

The t-score is a statistical measure of the likelihood that two or more words occur together by chance. It is a popular measure in corpus linguistics because compared with other measures it gives prominence to the very common words. To find out more about it, the paper by Stubbs (1995) is a good start. [Task 3]

TOKENISATION

The computer has problems with what is a word, and different corpora follow different conventions. In The Bank of English, it regards the shortened negative verbs like <u>can't</u> as two words, leaving <u>n't</u> as an English word, and curious forms like <u>ca</u> and <u>wo</u>. Whatever decision is taken produces results that do not entirely match our intuitions; this is because for users of English (and most languages) "word" is not a precisely defined notion. Humans do not face problems every few seconds as to what is a word; educated people have learned fairly consistent conventions for where to put word-spaces, and they do not consider whether hyphens or apostrophes divide words or just morphemes.

In grammar this causes occasional problems; the status of the possessive " 's" in English is very dubious; there are arguments for considering the so-called phrasal verbs like "look up" (meaning "consult") to be single words except that other words can come between the verb and the particle – and so on.

Suddenly we are in a complex area; the computer has no linguistic intuition and so has to be told everything precisely; the decisions we take at this early stage have far-reaching consequences and yet we do not want the computer's "word" to be too abstract a concept. This difference between the human way of seeing language and the machine one has to be remembered throughout corpus study, because it can affect our interpretations of the results of queries. [Task 11]

WORD

This is a general word in the language, and it would be confusing to try to allocate a precise definition to it. It covers the meanings of FORM, WORD FORM, LEMMA and HEADWORD in this book.

WORD FORM

See FORM. A string of characters between spaces in a text. This is the simplest item for the computer to search on, and contrasts with LEMMA, which is a collection of systematically related word forms that are thought to share the same meaning.